Hexed and Hallowed: THE TRUE STORY OF Witches

Then and Now

Hexed and Hallowed: The True Story of Witches, Then and Now

Robert J Dornan

All rights reserved. No part of this publication may be reproduced, distributed, or transmitted in any form or by any means, including photocopying, recording, or other electronic or mechanical methods, without the prior written permission of the publisher, except in the case of brief quotations embodied in critical reviews and certain other noncommercial uses permitted by copyright law.

This book is protected by copyright laws and international treaties. Unauthorized reproduction or distribution of this work, in whole or in part, constitutes a violation of the author's rights and is punishable by law.

Copyright © 2023 Robert J Dornan

Contents

Preface	VIII
1. Witchcraft Through the Ages: Unveiling the Enigmatic Past	1
2. Famous Witches in History: Legends and Legacy	4
3. Witch Hunts and Persecution: Dark Chapters in Witchcraft History	19
4. Witchcraft and Folklore: Myths, Legends, and Local Traditions	41
5. The Duality of Witches: Good vs. Evil in Witchcraft	44
6. Witches in Literature: From Macbeth to Modern Novels	47
7. The Covent of the Black Forest: Germany's 16th-Century Witches	50
8. The Mora Coven: Sweden's Infamous 17th-Century Witch Trials	54
9. The Coven of the Silver Moon	58
10. Witches in Pop Culture: Television, Film, and Fashion	61
11. Witchcraft and Feminism: Empowerment and Identity	65
12. Witchcraft and Community Traditions	68
13. Witchcraft and Healing: Herbalism, Remedies, and Modern Practices	71
14. Witchcraft and Shamanism: Exploring Altered States and Journeys	85

15.	Witchcraft and Ethics: Moral Codes and Responsible Magick	88
16.	Witchcraft and Nature Spirituality	91
17.	Witchcraft and Mediumship: Communicating with the Spirit World	94
18.	Witchcraft and Modern Spirituality: An Evolving Path	97
19.	Witchcraft and Sexuality: Unraveling the Mystical and Sensual	100
20.	Familiars and Spirit Animals: Allies in the Witch's Craft	105
21.	The Coven: Bonds, Roles, and Traditions	108
22.	Modern Witchcraft Movements: Eclectic Practices and New Traditions	111
23.	Witches, Religion, and Christianity: Intersections and Conflicts	114
24.	Spirit Work and Spirit Communication: Reaching Beyond the Veil	118
25.	Symbols and Rituals in Witchcraft: Tools and Traditions	121
26.	Meditation and Visualization: Inner Journeys in Witchcraft	187
27.	Male Witches: Breaking Stereotypes and Embracing Diversity	190
28.	Wicca: A Comprehensive Exploration of the Modern Witchcraft Religion	193
29.	Green Witches: Nature-Centric Practices and Eco-Spirituality	203
30.	Wiccan Protection Spell	224
31.	Wiccan Love Attraction Spell	227
32.	Wiccan Healing Spell	230
33.	Wiccan Prosperity Spell	234
34.	Wiccan Cleansing Spell	238
35.	Wiccan Protection Jar Spell	242
36.	Wiccan Banishing Spell	246

37.	Wiccan Moon Magic Spell	250
38.	Wiccan Divination Spell	254
39.	Wiccan Binding Spell	258
40.	Wiccan Self-Confidence spell	262
41.	Wiccan Communication Spell	266
42.	Wiccan Friendship Spell	270
43.	Wiccan Moon Magic Spell	274
44.	Wiccan Intuition Spell	278
45.	Wiccan Dream Protection Spell	282
46.	Wiccan Job or Career Spell	286
47.	Wiccan Breaking Bad Habits Spell	291
48.	Wiccan Creativity Spell	296
49.	Wiccan Travel Protection Spell	301
50.	Wiccan Ancestral Connection Spell	306
51.	Wiccan Empowerment Spell	310
52.	Wiccan Justice Spell	315
53.	Wiccan New Beginnings Spell	319
54.	Wiccan Gratitude Spell	324
55.	Robert J Dornan Books	328

Preface

Witches have haunted the imagination for centuries, shrouded in mystery, fear, and fascination. From the whispered accusations of medieval Europe to the dramatic trials of Salem, history has woven witches into the fabric of legend and reality. Still, beyond the darkened tales of persecution and pyres lies a deeper truth—a world of magic, wisdom, and resilience that continues to thrive today.

Hexed and Hallowed: The True Story of Witches, Then and Now takes you on a "spellbinding" journey through time, uncovering the evolution of witches from feared outcasts to empowered practitioners of modern spirituality. This reference book explores the infamous witch trials that gripped entire nations, the lives of legendary witches who defied societal norms, and the shifting perceptions that have shaped the image of witchcraft. It also discusses the principles of present-day witchcraft, revealing how modern witches harness the elements, practice healing, engage in mediumship, and embrace Wiccan traditions, (amongst others).

Whether you're drawn to the history of persecution, the magic of spells, or the cultural impact of witches in film and literature, *Hexed and Hallowed* offers an all-encompassing, 101-type look at the past and present of witchcraft. You are about to uncover the truth behind the myths, challenge the misconceptions, and open your eyes to the mystical world of those who dare to embrace the craft.

The magic is real—if you know where to look.

Chapter One

Witchcraft Through the Ages: Unveiling the Enigmatic Past

The history of witchcraft is a fascinating and complex subject that spans across different time periods and cultures. Exploring its origins and evolution sheds light on how beliefs, practices, and perceptions of witchcraft have evolved over time.

The origins of witchcraft can be traced back to ancient times, where beliefs in magic, divination, and the power of nature were prevalent. In many early societies, individuals known as witches, shamans, or wise women played important roles as healers, spiritual leaders, and advisors. They possessed knowledge of herbs, healing practices, and rituals that connected them to the spiritual realm.

Ancient Witchcraft

In ancient civilizations such as Mesopotamia, Egypt, and Greece, witchcraft and magic were deeply intertwined with religious practices. Magical spells, rituals, and divination techniques were performed to seek protection, healing, and guidance. For example, in ancient Greece, practitioners known as "pharmakides" used herbs and potions for healing purposes, while Egyptian priests and priestesses performed rituals to communicate with the gods.

Medieval Witchcraft

The medieval period marked a significant shift in the perception of witchcraft. With the spread of Christianity, witchcraft became associated with heresy and devil worship. The Church condemned practices that were considered outside the realm of orthodox Christianity, leading to the demonization of individuals believed to be involved in witchcraft. The infamous witch trials and persecutions occurred during this time, resulting in the execution of thousands of alleged witches.

European Witch Hunts

The height of the witch trials occurred between the 15th and 17th centuries, primarily in Europe. Fear, religious fervor, social unrest, and a belief in supernatural forces fueled the witch hunts. Accusations of witchcraft often targeted marginalized groups, particularly women, the elderly, and those who did not conform to societal norms. Methods of torture and coercion were used to extract confessions, and thousands of individuals, mostly women, were executed for crimes of witchcraft.

Modern Witchcraft Revival

The perception of witchcraft began to shift again in the 19th and 20th centuries with the rise of various spiritual and magical movements. The emergence of Wicca, founded by Gerald Gardner in the mid-20th century, marked a significant revival of witchcraft as a recognized religious and spiritual practice. Wicca emphasized a reverence for nature, the worship of a horned god and a triple goddess, and the use of ceremonial rituals and magic.

Contemporary Witchcraft

In modern times, witchcraft has gained broader acceptance and visibility. Contemporary witches often embrace eclectic practices, drawing inspiration from various spiritual traditions, folklore, and cultural beliefs. Many identify as Wiccans, pagans, or practitioners of modern witchcraft, incorporating rituals, spellcasting, divination, and the use of herbs, crystals, and tarot cards into their practices. The internet and social media have facilitated the exchange of knowledge and the formation of online communities for witches worldwide.

The history of witchcraft reveals the evolution of beliefs, practices, and societal attitudes towards witches. From revered healers and spiritual leaders in ancient times to the victims of persecution during the witch hunts, witches have played diverse roles. The revival and contemporary practice of witchcraft demonstrate its resilience and ongoing relevance as a spiritual path and a means of personal empowerment and connection to the natural world.

Chapter Two

Famous Witches in History: Legends and Legacy

Throughout human history, there have been several individuals who gained notoriety or were accused of practicing witchcraft. It's important to note that many of these individuals were victims of prejudice, superstition, and societal fears. Here are a few examples of famous witches from different periods:

The Witch of Endor (Old Testament)

Mentioned in the Bible, the Witch of Endor was summoned by King Saul of Israel to communicate with the spirit of the deceased prophet Samuel.

The Witch of Endor is a biblical figure mentioned in the First Book of Samuel in the Old Testament. She is known for her encounter with King Saul of Israel and her ability to summon the spirit of the deceased prophet Samuel. While the biblical account provides limited information about her life, here is a description based on the biblical narrative:

The Witch of Endor is believed to have been a woman residing in the town of Endor, located in the region of ancient Israel. Endor was situated on the slopes of Mount Tabor in the Jezreel Valley.

According to the biblical account, King Saul, who was troubled and facing an impending battle against the Philistines, sought guidance from God but received no response. Frustrated and desperate for answers, Saul sought out the Witch of Endor in secret.

The Witch of Endor was known for her ability to communicate with the spirits of the dead, which was considered a forbidden practice according to Jewish law. She possessed a reputation as a medium or necromancer, someone who could commune with the deceased.

When Saul approached her, disguised and seeking her assistance, she was initially hesitant due to the potential danger involved. However, Saul assured her that she would not be punished for her actions.

Following Saul's request, the Witch of Endor performed a ritual to summon the spirit of Samuel. To her surprise, the spirit of Samuel actually appeared before her and spoke to Saul, delivering a prophecy of Saul's impending downfall and the loss of his kingdom.

The exact identity and background of the Witch of Endor are not elaborated upon in the biblical text. She is simply depicted as a woman possessing supernatural abilities and knowledge in the realm of communing with spirits. Her actions were seen as blasphemous and condemned by the religious authorities of the time.

The story of the Witch of Endor exists within the context of religious and mythological narratives. Different interpretations and beliefs may vary, and the account of the Witch of Endor serves a specific purpose within the biblical story of King Saul's life and reign.

Circe (Greek Mythology)

A sorceress in Greek mythology, Circe was known for her ability to transform men into animals with her potions and spells. She is prominently featured in Homer's epic poem, "The Odyssey."

In Greek mythology, Circe is a powerful enchantress and sorceress known for her transformative abilities and encounters with various mythological heroes. Here's a description of Circe based on the myths and legends:

Circe is often depicted as a beautiful and captivating figure with an air of enchantment. She is the daughter of the sun god Helios and the nymph Perse, making her a nymph or a goddess in some interpretations. Circe is associated with magic, potions, and her ability to transform others.

One of the most famous stories involving Circe is her encounter with the hero Odysseus in Homer's epic poem, "The Odyssey." When Odysseus and his crew land on her island, Aeaea, Circe uses her magical powers to turn his companions into animals, most notably swine. However, she is intrigued by Odysseus' wit and intelligence, and rather than turning him into an animal, she becomes infatuated with him.

Circe is depicted as a skilled potion-maker and uses her knowledge of herbs and magic to create transformative potions. She is known for her ability to turn humans into animals or alter their forms. In some versions of the myth, she is also associated with the use of drugs and hallucinogens to achieve her magical effects.

Circe is a complex character who displays both benevolent and malevolent aspects. While she initially transforms Odysseus' crew, she later becomes an ally and lover of Odysseus, helping him on his journey and providing him with advice to continue his quest.

In addition to her encounters with Odysseus, Circe is often associated with other mythological figures, including the birth of famous Greek heroes such as Medea and the sons of Odysseus. She is sometimes portrayed as a seductress and temptress, luring men with her enchantments and captivating powers.

Overall, Circe is a figure of great magical prowess and allure. Her transformative abilities, association with potions and herbs, and complex interactions with mythological heroes make her a fascinating character within Greek mythology.

Morgan le Fay (Arthurian Legends)
Morgan le Fay is a character from Arthurian legends, often depicted as a powerful enchantress and sometimes portrayed as King Arthur's half-sister. She was associated with magic, healing, and shapeshifting.

Morgan le Fay is a prominent character in Arthurian legends and is often depicted as a powerful enchantress and sorceress. Here's a description of Morgan le Fay based on the various tales and interpretations within Arthurian lore:

Morgan le Fay, also known as Morgana, is often portrayed as a complex and multifaceted character. She is commonly depicted as a half-sister to King Arthur, usually through their shared mother, Igraine. However, her origins and parentage can vary in different versions of the legends.

Morgan le Fay possesses formidable magical abilities and is highly skilled in the arts of sorcery and enchantment. She is known for her powers of shapeshifting, healing, and manipulating the natural forces. Her magical abilities often make her a force to be reckoned with, and she is seen as one of the most skilled practitioners of magic in Arthurian mythology.

In many stories, Morgan le Fay is portrayed as a complex figure who oscillates between being an antagonist and a healer. While she is often depicted as a villainess, seeking to undermine Arthur and his knights, she is also shown as a healer and protector of the mystical island of Avalon. Some legends even suggest that she is one of the three enchantresses who take Arthur to Avalon after his last battle.

Morgan le Fay's motivations and actions can vary depending on the version of the myth. In some accounts, she seeks revenge against Arthur and his knights due to perceived wrongs done to her or her family. In others, she acts out of a desire for power or to protect the old Celtic traditions against the encroachment of Christianity.

Morgan le Fay is often portrayed as a beautiful and seductive woman who uses her charms and magical abilities to influence events and manipulate those around her. Her relationships with other Arthurian characters, such as her love affair with the knight Sir Lancelot, further add to her complexity and contribute to the intricate web of Arthurian mythology.

Overall, Morgan le Fay is a captivating and enigmatic figure in Arthurian legends. Her magical powers, conflicting motivations, and complicated relationships with other characters make her a compelling and enduring character within the Arthurian mythos.

The Pendle Witches (17th Century, England)
The Pendle Witches were a group of individuals accused and executed for witchcraft in Pendle Hill, Lancashire, England, in 1612. The trials and executions were part of the wider witch-hunting craze in England at the time.

The Pendle Witches were a group of individuals accused and executed for witchcraft in Pendle Hill, Lancashire, England, in 1612. Here's a description of the Pendle Witches based on historical accounts:

The Pendle Witches were mostly women, and their trials and executions were part of the wider witch-hunting craze that occurred in England during the 16th and 17th centuries. The events surrounding the Pendle Witch Trials have become one of the most famous and well-documented cases of witchcraft persecution in English history.

The main figures among the accused Pendle Witches were Elizabeth Device, her daughter Alizon Device, Anne Whittle (also known as Chattox), Anne Redferne, and Alice Nutter, among others. These women belonged to two rival families, the Devices and the Chattoxes, and were from impoverished backgrounds.

The accusations against the Pendle Witches arose from allegations of witchcraft, supernatural occurrences, and misfortune in the local area. It is said that the witches were believed to have made pacts with the devil and practiced malevolent magic against their neighbors.

The Pendle Witch Trials were conducted in a series of legal proceedings, with the accused witches appearing before the assize court in Lancaster. During the trials, testimonies were given by witnesses, including family members and neighbors who claimed to have experienced the witches' curses or seen them engaging in magical practices.

The accused witches were convicted based on the testimony and evidence presented against them. Some admitted to practicing witchcraft, while others maintained their innocence. The trials were conducted under the authority of the witchcraft laws of the time, which deemed witchcraft a criminal offense punishable by death.

In August 1612, ten of the Pendle Witches, including the main figures mentioned earlier, were executed by hanging on Gallows Hill in Lancaster. Their deaths marked the end of the Pendle Witch Trials.

The story of the Pendle Witches has gained significant attention and fascination over the years, and the trials have become an important part of Lancashire folklore and witchcraft history. They serve as a stark reminder of the fear, superstition, and hysteria that surrounded accusations of witchcraft during that era. Today, the legacy of the Pendle Witches continues to be remembered and explored through various historical accounts, literature, and cultural interpretations.

Tituba (Salem Witch Trials)

Tituba was a slave from Barbados and one of the first individuals accused of witchcraft during the Salem Witch Trials in colonial Massachusetts, USA, in 1692. Her confession and accusations played a significant role in sparking the trials.

Tituba is a significant figure in the context of the Salem Witch Trials that occurred in colonial Massachusetts in 1692. She was an enslaved woman of African descent who played a significant role in the accusations of witchcraft that ignited the hysteria and subsequent trials. Here's a description of Tituba based on historical records:

Tituba's origins and early life are not well-documented, but it is believed that she was brought to Massachusetts from Barbados, where she may have been enslaved. She was owned by Reverend Samuel Parris, a minister in Salem Village, which is now known as Danvers, Massachusetts.

During the winter of 1691-1692, a wave of mysterious and unexplained afflictions, including fits, seizures, and hallucinations, swept through the community, particularly affecting young girls. Seeking an explanation for these afflictions, Tituba, along with two other young girls in the Parris household, began engaging in folk magic and fortune-telling practices.

Under intense pressure from the local community to identify the cause of the afflictions, magistrates and ministers questioned Tituba. In her statements, she confessed to practicing witchcraft and implicated other individuals, fueling the escalating accusations of witchcraft in the community.

Tituba's confession had a significant impact on the course of events in the Salem Witch Trials. Her involvement and accusations set in motion a chain of events that led to the arrest and trials of numerous people in the community, resulting in the execution of twenty individuals.

The circumstances surrounding Tituba's confession and her role in the trials are complex. Some historians believe that her confession may have been coerced or influenced by her status as an enslaved woman and the power dynamics within the community. The extent of her actual involvement in witchcraft and her motives remain a subject of debate.

After her confession, Tituba was imprisoned, but her fate is uncertain. Some accounts suggest that she was eventually released from jail, while others suggest that she was sold or remained enslaved. Historical records provide limited information about her life after the trials.

Tituba's significance lies in her role as one of the initial individuals accused of witchcraft in the Salem Witch Trials. As a slave, her involvement highlighted the complex intersections of race, gender, and social dynamics during that period.

Her actions and accusations set in motion a tragic and tumultuous chapter in American history.

Marie Laveau (19th Century, New Orleans)

Marie Laveau was a prominent voodoo priestess and practitioner in New Orleans, Louisiana. She was known for her influence and spiritual work, providing guidance and healing to the community.

Marie Laveau was a prominent figure in the 19th century in New Orleans, particularly known for her association with Voodoo and her role as a practitioner and spiritual leader. Here's a description of Marie Laveau based on historical records and folklore:

Marie Laveau was born on September 10, 1801, in New Orleans, Louisiana. She was a free woman of African and French descent, with her heritage tracing back to both enslaved Africans and white colonizers. She became a prominent and influential figure within the Voodoo community in New Orleans during the 19th century.

Marie Laveau was known for her knowledge of African spiritual traditions, Catholicism, and local folk practices. She blended elements from these different belief systems to create her unique style of Voodoo that incorporated both African and Catholic rituals and symbolism. Her practices reflected the cultural syncretism that characterized New Orleans at the time.

As a Voodoo practitioner, Marie Laveau was believed to possess mystical abilities and was sought after for her spiritual guidance, healing, and divination skills. She was known for her accurate predictions and her ability to help in matters of love, luck, and protection.

Marie Laveau's reputation extended beyond the spiritual realm. She was recognized as a community leader and a social activist who used her influence to support and advocate for the rights of the African American community. She was known to have used her position to help enslaved individuals seek freedom and provided aid to those in need.

Laveau's influence and popularity were so widespread that she became a legendary figure in New Orleans, often referred to as the "Voodoo Queen" or the "Witch of New Orleans." Her tomb in St. Louis Cemetery No. 1 in New Orleans remains a popular pilgrimage site where visitors leave offerings and seek her blessings.

Much has been written and said about Marie Laveau and it is possible that the line between historical fact and folklore is severely blurred. Many stories and legends have surrounded her life, and separating truth from myth can be challenging. Nevertheless, Marie Laveau left an indelible mark on New Orleans and is remembered as a significant figure in the city's rich cultural and spiritual heritage.

Doreen Valiente (20th Century)
Doreen Valiente was a prominent figure in the modern witchcraft movement and played a significant role in the development and popularization of Wicca, particularly in the 20th century. The following summarizes her contributions and influence within the Wiccan community:

Doreen Valiente was born on January 4, 1922, in London, England. She is widely regarded as one of the most influential figures in the revival and modernization of witchcraft and Wicca. Valiente's interest in witchcraft began in her early years, and she became involved in various occult and magical traditions.

In the 1950s, Valiente became a member of Gerald Gardner's coven and played a crucial role in the development and codification of Wiccan rituals and practices. She worked closely with Gardner to document and refine the rituals and beliefs of Wicca, contributing significantly to the structure and formulation of modern Wiccan practices.

Valiente was an eloquent and poetic writer, and her contributions to Wiccan literature were instrumental in disseminating Wiccan teachings to a wider audience. She authored several books on witchcraft and Wicca, including "Witchcraft for Tomorrow" and "The Rebirth of Witchcraft." Her writings emphasized the importance of nature, magic, and the worship of the divine feminine in Wiccan spirituality.

Valiente also played a vital role in bringing historical accuracy and authenticity to the Wiccan tradition. She conducted extensive research into witchcraft folklore, mythology, and witch trials, seeking to root Wiccan practices in a rich historical and cultural context.

Beyond her literary contributions, Valiente was an advocate for religious freedom and worked to dispel misconceptions and prejudices surrounding witchcraft. She believed in the importance of accepting and celebrating diverse spiritual paths and was instrumental in gaining recognition and legal protection for Wicca as a legitimate religious practice in the United Kingdom.

Valiente's dedication to preserving the integrity of Wicca and her commitment to its ethical principles made her a highly respected figure within the Wiccan and wider pagan communities. Her influence continues to be felt in contemporary witchcraft, and her writings and teachings have inspired countless individuals to explore and embrace Wiccan spirituality.

Doreen Valiente's legacy as a pioneer, writer, and advocate for the modern witchcraft movement remains significant, and she is celebrated as one of the key figures in the development and popularization of Wicca in the 20th century.

Historical accounts and legends often blend fact and fiction, and the understanding of witches and their actions are glorified or ridiculed depending on cultural and societal perspectives. The perception of these individuals as witches is often rooted in the beliefs and fears of the time.

The Bell Witch

The legend of the Bell Witch began in the early 19th century in a quiet rural community just outside of Adams, Tennessee. John Bell, a respected farmer, found his family tormented by a malevolent force that would come to be known as the Bell Witch. According to legend, from 1817 to 1821, his family and the local area around Robertson County, came under attack by a mostly invisible entity that was able to speak, affect the physical environment, and shapeshift.

The strange happenings started subtly, with unexplained knocking on doors and walls, furniture moving on its own accord, and whispers in the dead of night. As time passed, the witch's presence grew bolder and more menacing. It targeted John Bell with ferocity, leaving him physically and mentally drained. His family and neighbors bore witness to his gradual decline, as the witch's attacks drained the life force from him. We say "it" because the entity presented herself in many forms.

In 1894, author Martin V. Ingram published a book about the Bell Witch claiming the entities name was Kate, after a dead neighbor – Kate Batts – who often complained that John Bell swindled her in a land purchase. In the beginning, the swarming by the entity centered on John Bell and his daughter, Betsy. He first event happened in 1817 with John Bell witnessing an apparition of a dog or something resembling a dog. He shot at the creature, but it disappeared. Many eerie events followed. Strange sounds filled the house at odd hours, including mysterious knocking, the sound of rats gnawing at bedposts, dogs barking and snarling, and chains being dragged across the floor. Bedsheets were torn from sleepers, and pillows were jerked from beneath their heads. Eventually, the Bells began to hear a woman's voice: the entity, it seemed, could talk, and she talked a *lot*. She knew scripture, and things about the family that no one else could know.

Word of the haunting spread, and the Bell family's home became a gathering place for the curious and the skeptical, all eager to witness the supernatural phenomena for themselves. The witch did not disappoint. Her actions escalated in intensity and malevolence. She would mimic voices, speaking in a twisted chorus, reciting biblical verses with mocking tones.

As the spirit's reign of terror continued, even the most skeptical of observers were forced to acknowledge the sinister reality of the situation. As per witnesses the witch possessed an awesome power, capable of inflicting physical harm to anyone she targeted. Visitors experienced scratching and bruising, even attacks by an invisible force, leaving them terrified and bewildered.

Numerous accounts from witnesses described the witch's spectral form appearing as a black dog, a rabbit, or a woman draped in a black shroud. It could be heard laughing and singing eerie melodies that echoed through the night, chilling the bones of those who heard them. It seemed to relish in the fear it instilled, feeding off the terror of its victims.

The witch's malevolence extended beyond the Bell family, targeting anyone who dared challenge its existence or try to rid the community of its presence. It unleashed chaos and terror, causing havoc in the lives of those who sought to defy it. Efforts to banish the witch through religious rituals and exorcisms proved futile, as the entity was impervious to conventional means of expulsion.

James Johnston, a family friend spent one night with the family and declared the entity was a "spirit, like in the Bible". When the word spread of the haunting, the witch became more extroverted and began to answer questions asked by tourists and townspeople and often shared gossip about county households.

Several outsiders and townsfolk tried to disprove the spectacular story of a witch and invisible entity but failed miserably. As per legend or hearsay, the malevolent spirit was not always evil. It showed signs of kindness, especially with John Bell's wife. As for Bell himself, she swore to kill him and sure enough, the patriarch was poisoned. At his funeral, the witch interrupted the service by singing drinking songs.

In a manuscript attributed to Richard Williams Bell, he wrote that the spirit remained a mystery:

Whether it was witchery, such as afflicted people in past centuries and the darker ages, whether some gifted fiend of hellish nature, practicing sorcery for selfish enjoyment, or some more modern science akin to that of mesmerism, or some hobgoblin native to the wilds of the country, or a disembodied soul shut out from heaven, or an evil spirit like those Paul [sic] drove out of the man into the swine, setting them mad; or a demon let loose from hell, I am unable to decide; nor has anyone yet divined its nature or cause for appearing, and I trust this description of the monster in all forms and shapes, and of many tongues, will lead experts who may come with a wiser generation, to a correct conclusion and satisfactory explanation.
—Williams Bell, An Authenticated History of the Bell Witch: Chapter 8

Numerous accounts from witnesses described the witch's spectral form appearing as a black dog, a rabbit, or a woman draped in a black shroud. It could be heard laughing and singing eerie melodies that echoed through the night, chilling the bones of those who heard them. It seemed to relish in the fear it instilled, feeding off the terror of its victims.

The witch's malevolence extended beyond the Bell family, targeting anyone who dared challenge its existence or try to rid the community of its presence. It unleashed chaos and terror, causing havoc in the lives of those who sought to defy it. Efforts to banish the witch through religious rituals and exorcisms proved futile, as the entity was impervious to conventional means of expulsion.

It wasn't until years later, after the death of John Bell, that the witch's torment finally ceased. Its parting words were both ominous and cryptic, promising to return in seven years. True to its word, seven years later, the witch did indeed make a reappearance, albeit in a more subdued manner and when the family chose to ignore its haunting, the entity disappeared never to return.

Several theories have emerged over the years concerning the Bell Witch hauntings. Some believe a local schoolteacher who was in love with Betsy Bell somehow fabricated the eerie phenomena so the girl would leave her betrothed and marry him instead. Modern day researchers and doubters believe that John Bell was slowly poisoned with arsenic by a family member or by one of his slaves.

As per the relation between the entity and witchery, the belief by most in Robertson County, was that the whole event was the evil doing of local witches who implanted visions and chanted rituals to avenge Kate Batts. No witch was persecuted for this sinister event.

To this day, the Bell Witch remains one of the most well-known and perplexing hauntings in American history. Its story has been passed down through generations, captivating the imagination of those who hear it. Other than a tourist trap called the Bell Witch Cave, Robertson County shares no association with the haunting. Even more fascinating, no one has been able to debunk the story other than to claim that the religious overtones of the era and environment set in motion an intentional manifestation.

Chapter Three

Witch Hunts and Persecution: Dark Chapters in Witchcraft History

Witch hunts and persecution refer to a dark chapter in history when individuals, primarily women, were accused, tried, and often executed for practicing witchcraft. The phenomenon of witch hunts occurred primarily during the Early Modern period, between the 15th and 18th centuries, but instances of witch persecution can be found throughout many cultures and time periods.

Origins of Witch Persecution

The origins of witch persecution can be traced back to a combination of factors including religious, societal, and cultural beliefs. The spread of Christianity in Europe played a significant role in shaping attitudes towards witchcraft. The Church condemned practices that were considered heretical or associated with devil worship, and witchcraft was seen as a threat to Christian orthodoxy. The belief in the existence of witches, their pact with the devil, and the ability to cause harm through malevolent magic became deeply ingrained in the collective consciousness.

Social and Cultural Factors

Witch persecution was not solely driven by religious motivations but was also influenced by social and cultural factors. During this period, society was characterized by fear, superstition, and a lack of scientific understanding. Widespread social unrest, economic hardships, and political instability created an atmosphere of anxiety and suspicion. In such a climate, individuals who deviated from societal norms or held unconventional beliefs became easy targets for accusations of witchcraft.

Accusations and Trials

Accusations of witchcraft were often based on flimsy evidence, gossip, and rumors. Women, especially older women, were particularly vulnerable to accusations due to their marginalized position in society. The accused were believed to have made a pact with the devil, participated in sabbats (gatherings of witches), and used magic to cause harm to others. Torture was commonly employed to extract confessions, leading to the accused confessing to crimes they did not commit.

Witch Trials and Execution

Witch trials were conducted in various forms, depending on the region and legal systems in place. These trials were often characterized by biased judges, lack of due process, and the presumption of guilt. In many cases, the accused were denied legal representation and subjected to unfair interrogation methods. The punishment for being found guilty of witchcraft ranged from public humiliation, torture, and imprisonment to execution, with burning at the stake being one of the most infamous methods.

There were several notable witch trials throughout history, apart from the Salem Witch Trials. Here are some famous witch trials:

The Pendle Witch Trials (1612)
The Pendle Witch Trials were a series of witchcraft trials that took place in Pendle Hill, Lancashire, England, in 1612. These trials were among the most famous and significant witch trials in English history, and they resulted in the execution of ten people, including nine women and one man. The Pendle Witch Trials are often regarded as a notable example of the persecution and hysteria surrounding witchcraft during the 17th century.

The events leading up to the trials began in March 1612 when a young girl named Alizon Device encountered a peddler named John Law in the forest near Pendle Hill. It was reported that Alizon, in a moment of anger, cursed Law after a dispute. Shortly after, Law suffered a stroke and attributed his illness to Alizon's curse. This incident, along with other rumors of witchcraft in the area, led to the arrest of Alizon and her family members, who were believed to be involved in witchcraft.

The trials were conducted at Lancaster Assizes, a court held at Lancaster Castle. The main figures on trial were members of two rival families: the Demdike family, headed by Elizabeth Southerns (also known as Old Demdike), and the Device family, led by James Device. Elizabeth Southerns, along with her daughter Elizabeth Device, her grandchildren James and Alizon Device, and other associates, were accused of various acts of witchcraft.

During the trials, the accused were interrogated and subjected to intense scrutiny. Witnesses, including family members and neighbors, testified against them, recounting alleged instances of witchcraft, including curses, spells, and meetings with the Devil. It is worth noting that the testimonies were often based on hearsay and superstition, fueled by a climate of fear and paranoia surrounding witchcraft.

The trials garnered significant public attention, and the accused witches were seen as a threat to society. The legal proceedings were far from fair, and the outcome seemed predetermined, as confessions were obtained under duress and coercion. Many of the accused confessed to their alleged crimes, likely to avoid further torture or execution.

Ten individuals were found guilty of witchcraft and sentenced to death. On August 20, 1612, nine women—Elizabeth Southerns (Old Demdike), Elizabeth Device, Anne Whittle (Chattox), Anne Redferne, Alice Nutter, Katherine Hewitt, Jane Bulcock, Alice Gray, and Jennet Preston—were hanged on Gallows Hill in Lancaster. Thomas Potts, the clerk of the court, documented the trials and published a detailed account titled "The Wonderfull Discoverie of Witches in the Countie of Lancaster."

The Pendle Witch Trials had a lasting impact on English society, serving as a chilling reminder of the dangers of religious and social paranoia. They highlighted the vulnerability of marginalized individuals, particularly women, who were often targets of witchcraft accusations. The trials also contributed to the broader narrative of witchcraft persecution in Europe and the New World during the early modern period.

In recent years, the Pendle Witch Trials have gained renewed interest and become a popular tourist attraction. The area around Pendle Hill is associated with witchcraft folklore, and visitors can explore the historical sites and learn more about the events that unfolded during that tumultuous period.

The North Berwick Witch Trials (1590-1592)

The North Berwick Witch Trials were a series of witchcraft trials that took place in the town of North Berwick, Scotland, between 1590 and 1592. These trials are one of the most significant and influential witch trials in Scottish history. The events surrounding the trials were marked by accusations of witchcraft, sorcery, and alleged involvement in a conspiracy against King James VI of Scotland (who later became James I of England).

The trials were rooted in the witch-hunting fervor that swept through Europe during the late 16th and early 17th centuries. The town of North Berwick, located on the east coast of Scotland, was believed to be a hotbed of witchcraft and supernatural activity. It was believed that a coven of witches, led by Agnes Sampson, a local healer and midwife, engaged in various acts of sorcery and made pacts with the Devil.

The trials were initiated after the King's ship encountered a series of storms while returning to Scotland from Denmark, where James VI's marriage to Princess Anne of Denmark had taken place. The King became convinced that witchcraft was responsible for the storms and sought to uncover the alleged conspiracy against him.

Agnes Sampson was one of the first individuals to be arrested and brought to trial. She was subjected to brutal torture, including sleep deprivation, witch pricking, and the infamous "waking" or "witnessing" torture. Under this extreme duress, Sampson confessed to various acts of witchcraft, including attending a witches' sabbat, casting spells, and attempting to murder the King through supernatural means.

Sampson's confession implicated several other individuals, leading to a wave of arrests and trials. Many of those accused were prominent members of society, including members of the nobility, clergymen, and townspeople. The trials involved the use of both physical and spectral evidence, with witnesses testifying to witnessing the accused participating in dark rituals and consorting with demons in their spectral forms.

The trials attracted significant attention and became widely known across Scotland. James VI himself took a keen interest in the proceedings and even personally examined some of the accused. The trials resulted in numerous convictions and subsequent executions. Many of those found guilty were burned at the stake, while others were imprisoned or banished.

The North Berwick Witch Trials had a profound impact on Scottish society and contributed to the overall climate of fear and paranoia surrounding witchcraft at the time. They played a significant role in shaping King James VI's attitudes towards witchcraft, eventually leading to the publication of his influential work, "Daemonologie," in 1597. This treatise served as a justification for the persecution of witches and played a part in the subsequent English witch trials during James's reign as King of England.

The trials also left a legacy in Scottish history and folklore. The North Berwick area is still associated with witchcraft, and there are various sites and landmarks linked to the trials that attract tourists and those interested in the occult. The events of the North Berwick Witch Trials serve as a stark reminder of the dangers of mass hysteria, the power of superstition, and the devastating consequences of witch-hunting during that era.

The Basque Witch Trials (1609-1614)

The Basque Witch Trials, also known as the Basque Witch Persecutions, were a series of witchcraft trials that took place in the Basque Country, a region spanning parts of northern Spain and southwestern France, during the 17th century. While not as widely known as some of the other witch trials of the era, the Basque Witch Trials were a significant episode of witch-hunting in the Iberian Peninsula.

The trials occurred against the backdrop of widespread beliefs in witchcraft and the existence of witches as malevolent practitioners of magic. The Basque Country, with its distinct cultural and linguistic heritage, was no exception to these beliefs. The trials were driven by a combination of religious fervor, fear, and superstition prevalent during that time.

The exact timeline and details of the Basque Witch Trials are fragmented and scarce due to limited documentation. However, it is known that witch trials occurred in various Basque towns and villages, including Zugarramurdi, Navarra, and the Baztan Valley. These trials were often carried out by local ecclesiastical and secular authorities.

One of the most infamous episodes associated with the Basque Witch Trials is the Witch Trials of Zugarramurdi, which took place in the late 16th and early 17th centuries. Zugarramurdi, a small village in Navarra, became known as a hub of witchcraft and satanic practices. The trials in Zugarramurdi were marked by numerous accusations, interrogations, and confessions extracted under duress and torture.

The accused were mainly women, although some men were also implicated. The trials focused on allegations of witchcraft, black magic, and participation in satanic rituals. The accused were believed to have made pacts with the Devil, engaged in shapeshifting, and used spells and curses to cause harm to others. The trials often involved detailed testimonies of witnesses who claimed to have witnessed the witches' gatherings, the use of potions, and various supernatural acts.

Torture was commonly employed to extract confessions from the accused, with methods such as the strappado (where the victim's hands were tied behind their back, and they were suspended in the air by a rope) and waterboarding being employed. Confessions obtained through such means were then used as evidence against the accused during the trials.

The Basque Witch Trials resulted in numerous convictions, with many accused witches being executed, typically by burning at the stake. The trials brought about widespread fear and paranoia in the region, and the witch-hunting fervor continued for some time, albeit with diminishing intensity.

In recent years, there has been renewed interest in the Basque Witch Trials, particularly the events in Zugarramurdi. The village has become a site of pilgrimage for those interested in witchcraft and occult history, and a museum dedicated to the trials has been established.

The Basque Witch Trials reflect the broader European phenomenon of witch trials during the early modern period, characterized by religious persecution, superstition, and the demonization of marginalized groups, particularly women. While the exact number of victims and details of the trials remain unclear, the trials serve as a reminder of the dangers of mass hysteria, the power of fear, and the devastating consequences of witch-hunting in history.

The Roermond Witch Trials (1613-1615)

These infamous trials are only known about because of a pamphlet. The actual process papers have been lost. 64 witches were arrested. The charges were: miscarriages, diseases in animals and fish, diseases in crops, and many people losing their livelihood. The witches had allegedly bewitched all these people. The charges no longer came from the peasants, but from the church and government who had investigated the complaints themselves and made the charges.

There was now a true inquisition. The accusations were not only of bewitchings but also of heresy and forming a pact with the devil and having danced and had intercourse with him. The witches were forced by means of torture to reveal the names of other witches that had partaken in the sabbath. Giving up the names of other witches was the main cause of the large number of trials.

Tryntjen van Zittaert was the first to be arrested, together with her daughter, who learned witchcraft from her. While playing with children on the street she was said to have showed her crafts to other children.

The 12-year-old girl magically made things appear out of her mouth, like coins. A magistrate noticed and mother and daughter were taken into custody. The girl said she had learned everything from her mother. Both were from Sittard, where things like prestidigitation were allowed, but in the more Protestant Roermond this was not tolerated.

Tryntjen was tortured and admitted to killing forty-one children with magic, and three men and seven women, and many crops and animals. She also accused the surgeon Jan van Ool of being a wizard. This Jan van Ool was from Gulik which was also less strictly religious than Roermond. After four days in custody the mother was burnt to death, and the daughter was locked into a convent for the rest of her life.

The ten other witches were taken into custody together with Jan van Ool. He admitted to having tried to convince his wife to seal a pact with the devil, which she refused. He claimed he then became scared she would turn him in, so he cut her into pieces and threw her down a well and told everyone she ran away. The devil forced him to kill one patient with magic for every ten he healed. In sixteen years, he would have killed 150 people. That would mean he would be treating about one hundred people a year. During his torture he accused forty-one other people of being witches. He was burnt alive.

These forty-one alleged witches were also taken into custody. They admitted to having killed children, crippled or diseased people, including their own families. They said they had been forced into these actions by the devil.

Near Straelen the magistrates arrested another ten alleged witches, who in their turn accused a midwife named Entjen Gillis.

Entjen Gillis confessed to having killed the fetuses of forty pregnant women, and 150 babies just after birth. She had also supposedly killed their mothers and her husband and children with witchcraft. She was burnt alive.

Altogether there were sixty-three witches and Jan van Ool, so during a month two people were burnt to the stake every day. The trials were handled in a noticeably abbreviated period of time. The magistrates decided this needed to be done because over six hundred newborn children and four hundred elderly, as well as over six thousand animals were killed by witchcraft.

The Bamberg Witch Trials (1623-1633)

The Bamberg Witch Trials were a series of witchcraft trials that took place in the city of Bamberg, in what is now modern-day Germany, between 1626 and 1631. These trials were one of the largest and most notorious witch trials in German history. The events in Bamberg were marked by a climate of religious fervor, social unrest, and the widespread belief in witchcraft and the Devil's influence.

The trials were conducted in the context of the Thirty Years' War, a devastating conflict that ravaged Europe, including the Holy Roman Empire. The war created an atmosphere of fear and uncertainty, with people seeking explanations for the turmoil and devastation. This atmosphere provided fertile ground for the growth of witch-hunting and the persecution of those suspected of witchcraft.

The witch trials in Bamberg were initiated by Prince-Bishop Johann Georg II Fuchs von Dornheim, who was known for his strong belief in the existence of witches and his dedication to eradicating witchcraft from his territory. Under his authority, a special witch-hunting commission was established, composed of clergy, magistrates, and legal experts.

The trials began with a wave of arrests and interrogations. The accused were mostly women, although men were also targeted. The trials focused on accusations of witchcraft, sorcery, and compacts with the Devil. The accused were believed to have made pacts with the Devil, attended witches' Sabbaths, and engaged in malevolent acts such as casting spells, causing illness, and harming livestock and crops.

The accused were subjected to harsh interrogation methods, including torture, to extract confessions. Common forms of torture included the strappado (a painful suspension by the wrists), the rack (a stretching device), and water torture. Confessions obtained through torture were often used as evidence in the trials.

The trials in Bamberg resulted in many convictions and subsequent executions. The exact number of victims is unclear, but estimates range from several hundred to over a thousand. The accused were typically executed by burning at the stake, a common method of execution for those found guilty of witchcraft during this period.

The trials in Bamberg attracted attention both within the region and beyond. They were regarded as particularly brutal and severe, even by the standards of the time. The trials in Bamberg became a symbol of the excesses and injustices of the witch-hunting frenzy that swept across Europe during the early modern period.

Over time, attitudes towards witchcraft shifted, and the fervor for witch trials began to wane. In 1631, the Thirty Years' War reached Bamberg, leading to the interruption of the trials. The war disrupted the operations of the witch-hunting commission, and the trials gradually ended.

The Bamberg Witch Trials left a lasting impact on the city's history and collective memory. The events served as a dark reminder of the dangers of mass hysteria, religious fanaticism, and the persecution of marginalized groups. Today, Bamberg acknowledges its historical involvement in the witch trials, and the city has memorialized the victims as part of efforts to remember and learn from this tragic chapter in its past.

The Great Scottish Witch Hunt (1661-1662)

The Great Scottish Witch Hunt refers to a period of intense persecution and trials of individuals accused of witchcraft in Scotland, which took place during the late 16th and early 17th centuries. It is considered one of the most significant and brutal witch-hunting episodes in Scottish history.

The hunt began in the 1590s and continued until the early 1660s, covering multiple regions across Scotland. It was characterized by a combination of religious, political, and social factors that contributed to a climate of fear and paranoia regarding witchcraft and demonic influence.

Religion played a crucial role in shaping the witch hunt. The Protestant Reformation had brought significant changes to Scotland, with the country transitioning from Catholicism to Protestantism. Protestant theologians and church leaders believed in the literal existence of witches and saw them as agents of Satan who posed a threat to the newly established Protestant faith.

Additionally, political instability and a lack of central authority during this period heightened anxieties. Scotland experienced internal conflicts and tensions between various factions, which further contributed to the search for scapegoats and the persecution of those suspected of practicing witchcraft.

The witch hunt was marked by widespread accusations, trials, and executions. Accusations often stemmed from allegations of malevolent acts, such as causing harm to people or livestock, practicing harmful magic, or making pacts with the Devil. Many accusations were driven by personal rivalries, grudges, or even attempts to seize property or inheritances from the accused.

Trials and interrogations were often conducted without due process or legal protections for the accused. The use of torture to extract confessions was prevalent, with methods including sleep deprivation, strappado, and waterboarding. Confessions obtained through such means were used as evidence in court, leading to further convictions and executions.

The accused were mostly women, although men were also targeted. Most of those accused were from lower social classes, including peasants and widows, although individuals from various walks of life were also implicated. The hunts often targeted marginalized individuals, such as healers, midwives, and those perceived as different or non-conformist.

The punishments for those found guilty of witchcraft were severe. Convicted witches were typically burned at the stake, although other methods of execution, such as hanging, were also employed. The authorities often seized properties and possessions of the accused.

The Great Scottish Witch Hunt gradually declined in the mid-17th century, partly due to changing attitudes and a growing skepticism towards the reality of witchcraft. The passage of the Witchcraft Act of 1649 introduced more stringent requirements for evidence, which made it harder to secure convictions. The final significant witch trial in Scotland took place in 1662, marking the end of this period of intense persecution.

The legacy of the Great Scottish Witch Hunt is still felt in Scotland today. It left a profound impact on Scottish society, contributing to a climate of fear, distrust, and superstition that persisted for generations. The hunts highlighted the dangers of mass hysteria, religious fanaticism, and the persecution of marginalized groups, particularly women, who were disproportionately targeted.

In recent years, there has been increased recognition of the victims of the witch hunts, with efforts to remember and memorialize those who suffered. Scotland has taken steps to acknowledge this dark period in its history and learn from it, ensuring that the victims are not forgotten and promoting a more inclusive and tolerant society.

The Würzburg Witch Trials (1626-1631)
The Würzburg Witch Trials were a series of witchcraft trials that occurred in the city of Würzburg, in present-day Germany, from 1626 to 1631. This period marked one of the most intense and brutal witch-hunting episodes in the history of the Holy Roman Empire.

The trials in Würzburg were initiated by Prince-Bishop Philipp Adolf von Ehrenberg, who held both religious and secular authority in the region. The bishop was deeply influenced by the Catholic Counter-Reformation, which viewed witchcraft as a grave threat to the Church and society.

Under the bishop's authority, a special witch-hunting commission was established to investigate and prosecute those accused of witchcraft. The commission was composed of theologians, lawyers, and local officials, all of whom were fervently committed to eradicating witchcraft from the region.

The trials began with a wave of arrests and interrogations. The accused were mostly women, although men were also targeted. The trials focused on accusations of witchcraft, black magic, and demonic pacts. The accused were believed to have made agreements with the Devil, attended witches' Sabbaths, and engaged in malevolent acts such as casting spells, causing illness, and harming crops and livestock.

The accused were subjected to harsh interrogation methods, including physical torture, to extract confessions. These methods included the strappado (a form of suspension by the wrists), water torture, and the use of thumbscrews. Confessions obtained through torture were often used as evidence during the trials.

The Würzburg Witch Trials resulted in many convictions and subsequent executions. The exact number of victims is difficult to determine, but estimates suggest that several hundred people, primarily women, were executed. The accused were typically burned at the stake, although some were also beheaded or hanged.

The trials in Würzburg were marked by their extreme cruelty and the high number of executions. The witch-hunting commission was known for its zeal and its willingness to employ any means necessary to secure convictions. The trials were swift, with little regard for due process, and the accused were often denied legal representation or the opportunity to present a defense.

The trials gained notoriety both within the region and beyond. They were considered one of the most savage and oppressive witch-hunting episodes of the time. The events in Würzburg contributed to a climate of fear and paranoia, with neighbors often accusing each other and the accused being forced to name others during their own trials, perpetuating the cycle of accusations and persecutions.

The Würzburg Witch Trials ended with the intervention of secular authorities. In 1631, the city of Würzburg was besieged and occupied by Swedish forces during the Thirty Years' War. The Swedish military commander, Bernhard of

Saxe-Weimar, put an end to the witch trials and disbanded the witch-hunting commission.

In August 1629, the Chancellor of the Prince-Bishop of Würzburg wrote the following to a friend:

As to the affair of the witches, which Your Grace thinks brought to an end before this, it has started up afresh, and no words can do justice to it. Ah, the woe and the misery of it--there are still four hundred in the city, high and low, of every rank and sex, nay, even clerics, so strongly accused that they may be arrested at any hour. It is true that, of the people of my Gracious Prince here, some out of all offices and faculties must be executed: clerics, electoral councilors and doctors, city officials, court assessors, several of whom Your Grace knows. There are law students to be arrested. The Prince-Bishop has over forty students who are soon to be pastors; among them thirteen or fourteen are said to be witches. A few days ago, a Dean was arrested; two others who were summoned have fled. The notary of our Church consistory, a very learned man, was yesterday arrested and put to the torture. In a word, a third part of the city is surely involved. The richest, most attractive, most prominent, of the clergy are already executed. A week ago, a maiden of nineteen was executed, of whom it is everywhere said that she was the fairest in the whole city and was held by everybody a girl of singular modesty and purity. She will be followed by seven or eight others of the best and most attractive persons ... And thus, many are put to death for renouncing God and being at the witch-dances, against whom nobody has ever else spoken a word.

To conclude this wretched matter, there are children of three and four years, to the number of three hundred, who are said to have had intercourse with the Devil. I have seen put to death children of seven, promising students of ten, twelve, fourteen, and fifteen. Of the nobles--but I cannot and must not write more of this misery. There are persons of yet higher rank, whom you know, and would marvel to hear of, nay, would scarcely believe it; let justice be done.

P. S. -- Though there are many wonderful and terrible things happening, it is beyond doubt that, at a place called the Fraw-Rengberg, the Devil in person, with eight thousand of his followers, held an assembly and celebrated mass before them all, administering to his audience (that is, the witches) turnip-rinds and parings in place of the Holy Eucharist. There took place not only foul but most horrible and hideous blasphemies, whereof I shudder to write. It is also true that they all vowed not to be enrolled in the Book of Life, but all agreed to be inscribed by a notary who is well known to me and my colleagues. We hope, too, that the book in which they are enrolled will yet be found, and there is no little search being made for it.

The legacy of the Würzburg Witch Trials is a dark chapter in the history of the city and the region. The events highlight the dangers of mass hysteria, religious fanaticism, and the persecution of marginalized groups, particularly women. Today, Würzburg acknowledges its historical involvement in the witch trials and strives to remember the victims to learn from the past and promote tolerance and justice.

These are just a few examples of the numerous witch trials that took place throughout history. Each trial had its unique circumstances and consequences, but they collectively serve as reminders of the dangers of mass hysteria, prejudice, and the abuse of power. Then of course, there were the Salem Witch Trials

Salem Witch Trials

One of the most well-known examples of witch persecution is the Salem Witch Trials that took place in colonial Massachusetts, United States, in 1692. Accusations of witchcraft were made against several individuals, leading to a mass hysteria and the execution of 20 people. The Salem witch trials serve as a stark reminder of the devastating consequences of false accusations, religious zealotry, and mass hysteria.

Context: The Salem Witch Trials occurred during a time when the beliefs in witchcraft and the supernatural were prevalent in Europe and its colonies. Puritanism was the dominant religious and social ideology in Salem, and the community was highly religious and strict in their interpretation of Christianity.

Accusations: The trials began with accusations of witchcraft made against several young girls in Salem Village. These girls exhibited unusual behavior, including fits, convulsions, and claiming to be possessed by witches. They accused others, mainly women, of practicing witchcraft and causing their afflictions.

Fear and Hysteria: The accusations sparked widespread fear and hysteria within the community. People became suspicious of their neighbors, and paranoia spread rapidly. The fear of witches and the devil infiltrating the community led to a climate of suspicion, finger-pointing, and accusations.

Trials and Legal Process: The accused witches were brought to trial in a court of law. The trials were marked by unfair procedures, including spectral evidence (testimony about alleged supernatural encounters) and the assumption of guilt unless proven innocent. The legal process was heavily influenced by superstition, religious beliefs, and societal pressures.

Accused and Victims: Most of the accused were women, although men were also targeted. Accusations were often directed at those who were considered socially marginalized, such as widows, older women, or those with unconventional behavior. Many of the accused were innocent, but under the pressure of the trials, some confessed to witchcraft to save themselves.

Executions: The Salem Witch Trials resulted in the execution of twenty individuals, fourteen women, and six men. They were executed by hanging, while one man, Giles Corey, was pressed to death with heavy stones. Several others died in jail due to harsh conditions or while awaiting trial.

Aftermath and Reflection: The trials eventually lost momentum as the accusations became more extreme and the community began to question the validity of the witchcraft claims. In 1693, the colonial government disbanded the court responsible for the trials, and those remaining in jail were released. The Salem Witch Trials left a lasting impact on American history, serving as a cautionary tale about the dangers of mass hysteria, religious extremism, and the erosion of due process.

Historical Significance: The Salem Witch Trials have been studied and analyzed extensively in the fields of history, sociology, psychology, and law. They serve as a reminder of the dangers of intolerance, the power of fear, and the consequences of unchecked hysteria. The trials have sparked ongoing discussions about gender, power dynamics, religious fervor, and the importance of protecting individual rights.

It is important to note that the Salem Witch Trials were a specific historical event that occurred within a particular cultural and social context. They should not be confused with modern witchcraft practices or the contemporary Wiccan religion, which emerged centuries later and have distinct beliefs and practices.

Legacy and Historical Perspective: The witch hunts and persecution left a lasting impact on society, contributing to the demonization of women, the suppression of alternative beliefs, and the perpetuation of stereotypes and fear surrounding witchcraft. It took centuries for the perception of witches to gradually shift from malevolent beings to figures associated with empowerment, nature, and spirituality. The tragic history of witch hunts serves as a reminder of the dangers of prejudice, intolerance, and the abuse of power.

The Medieval Inquisition

The Medieval Inquisition, specifically concerning the persecution of witches, was a dark and troubling chapter in history. It was a period marked by widespread fear, superstition, and religious fervor, during which individuals, primarily women, were accused of practicing witchcraft and subjected to severe punishment, including torture and execution. Here is an extensive description of the Medieval Inquisition of witches:

Background:

The Inquisition, established by the Catholic Church in the 13th century, was initially created to combat heresy and ensure religious orthodoxy. However, as the belief in witchcraft and the fear of Satan's influence grew, the focus of the Inquisition extended to include the investigation and eradication of alleged witches. This shift in focus led to the rise of witch trials and the systematic persecution of individuals accused of witchcraft.

Accusations and Trials:

Accusations of witchcraft were often based on superstition, folklore, hearsay, and personal grudges. Many accusers believed that witches made pacts with the Devil, possessed supernatural powers, and engaged in malevolent practices such as casting spells, causing harm, and participating in sabbaths.

The accused were subjected to trials, which were often biased, lacking in due process, and heavily influenced by the prevailing belief in witchcraft. The accused faced a daunting legal system, where they were presumed guilty and forced to prove their innocence. The trials were riddled with ignorance, hysteria, and the use of questionable evidence, such as spectral testimonies, witch's marks, and confessions obtained through torture.

Torture and Interrogation:

Torture was commonly employed during the Inquisition to extract confessions and gather evidence against accused witches. Techniques such as the strappado (suspending the accused by their wrists with weights tied to their ankles), the rack (stretching the accused's limbs), and the water torture (forcing water into the accused's mouth to simulate drowning) were used to elicit confessions, even though such confessions were often false and obtained under duress.

Punishments and Execution:
Once found guilty, the punishments for witches were severe and gruesome. Common forms of execution included burning at the stake, hanging, or, in some cases, being drowned. These punishments were not only meant to eradicate the supposed evil but also to serve as a deterrent to others who might consider engaging in witchcraft.

Social Impact and Legacy:
The persecution of witches during the Medieval Inquisition had a significant impact on society. It created an atmosphere of fear, suspicion, and paranoia, leading to the scapegoating and victimization of vulnerable individuals, particularly women. The hysteria surrounding witchcraft contributed to the erosion of civil liberties and human rights, as well as the reinforcement of patriarchal norms and power structures.

The legacy of the Medieval Inquisition and the witch trials is one of tragedy and injustice. Countless innocent lives were lost, families were torn apart, and communities were shattered due to the unfounded accusations and fervent belief in witchcraft. It serves as a chilling reminder of the dangers of unchecked power, mass hysteria, and the potential for human cruelty in the name of religion and fear.

Witch hunts and persecution represent a dark period in history when countless individuals, primarily women, were unjustly accused, tried, and often executed based on superstitions, fear, and societal anxieties. Understanding the historical context, social factors, and long-lasting impact of witch persecution is crucial in fostering tolerance in our present day society. By learning from the past, society can strive to create a more inclusive and accepting future.

Chapter Four

Witchcraft and Folklore: Myths, Legends, and Local Traditions

Witchcraft and folklore are intertwined aspects of human culture that have existed for centuries. They encompass a wide range of beliefs, practices, and traditions that are passed down through generations. Here is an extensive description of witchcraft and folklore:

Beliefs and Perspectives:

The beliefs surrounding witchcraft vary significantly from one country to another and from one era to another. In some traditions, witches are revered as spiritual leaders, healers, or wise individuals who possess deep knowledge of nature and the mystical arts. They are often regarded as intermediaries between the human and spiritual realms. In other cultures, witches may be feared and associated with malevolence, often depicted as practitioners of dark magic or in league with malevolent entities.

Folklore: Folklore encompasses the traditional customs, stories, legends, and beliefs of a particular community or culture. It is the oral and written tradition that is passed down through generations, often shaping the cultural identity and worldview of a group of people. Folklore encompasses various elements, including m Popular witch folklore stories, fairy tales, and myths have captured the imagination of people for generations. Here are descriptions of some well-known tales:

"Hansel and Gretel": This Brothers Grimm fairy tale follows the story of two children who stumble upon a witch's gingerbread house in the forest. The witch, who lures children to her home to eat them, is eventually outsmarted by the clever siblings.

"Snow White": In this classic fairy-tale, Snow White encounters an evil queen who disguises herself as a witch to harm the young princess. The queen uses a poisoned apple to put Snow White into a deep sleep until she is awakened by true love's kiss.

"The Wizard of Oz": Although not solely focused on witches, this beloved story features the Wicked Witch of the West as the primary antagonist. Dorothy and her companions face various challenges and encounters with magical beings on their journey to find the Wizard.

"Macbeth": This tragedy by William Shakespeare portrays the character of the Three Witches, also known as the Weird Sisters, who prophesy Macbeth's rise to power and subsequent downfall. Their dark and mysterious presence adds an element of supernatural intrigue to the play.

"The Witch of Endor": This biblical story, found in the First Book of Samuel, recounts the encounter between King Saul and the Witch of Endor. Saul seeks the witch's help to communicate with the spirit of the deceased prophet Samuel.

"The Legend of Baba Yaga": Baba Yaga is a prominent figure in Slavic folklore. She is a fearsome witch who dwells in a hut that stands on chicken legs and is known for her unusual appearance and unpredictable behavior. She often tests the bravery and wit of those who cross her path.

"The Legend of Morgan le Fay": Morgan le Fay is a powerful enchantress and antagonist in Arthurian legends. She is often depicted as a sorceress and half-sister to King Arthur, using her magical abilities to influence events in the Arthurian realm.

"The Blair Witch Project": This modern folklore tale is a found-footage horror film that revolves around the legend of the Blair Witch, a malevolent witch believed to haunt the Black Hills Forest in Maryland. The film's realistic and chilling portrayal of a witch's curse has captivated audiences worldwide.

These are just a few examples of popular witch folklore stories, fairy tales, and myths. They illustrate the varied and sometimes contrasting portrayals of witches, ranging from evil and malevolent beings to wise and mysterious figures. These tales continue to enchant and entertain, shaping our understanding and perception of witches in popular culture.

Role of Witches in Folklore:
Witches play a prominent role in folklore worldwide, appearing in various tales, legends, and myths. They are often depicted as powerful beings with supernatural abilities, both for good and evil purposes. In folklore, witches may be portrayed as wise old women, enchantresses, shapeshifters, or figures with a connection to the natural world. Their stories often revolve around themes of transformation, magic, and the consequences of meddling with the supernatural.

Chapter Five

The Duality of Witches: Good vs. Evil in Witchcraft

The concepts of "good witches" and "bad witches" are prevalent in folklore, literature, and popular culture. These terms are often associated with witches and their behavior, morals, and intentions. Here's a detailed description of what comprises a good witch and a bad witch:

Good Witch

Morality and Ethics: Good witches are typically characterized by their strong moral compass and ethical behavior. They use their magical powers for benevolent purposes, such as helping others, healing the sick, and protecting their communities. They adhere to a strict code of conduct that guides their actions.

Intentions: Good witches have positive intentions. They use their magic to bring about positive change, promote harmony, and maintain balance in the natural world. Their spells and actions are aimed at making the world a better place.

Healing and Protection: Many good witches are known for their ability to heal and protect. They may create potions, charms, or rituals to cure illnesses, ward off evil, or offer guidance to those in need.

Respect for Nature: Good witches often have a deep respect for nature and its elements. They work in harmony with the environment and seek to preserve the balance of the natural world. They may be herbalists, gardeners, or environmental activists.

Altruism: Good witches are typically selfless and altruistic. They are willing to use their powers to help others, even at personal cost. They may serve as wise advisors or healers within their communities.

Guidance and Wisdom: Good witches are often seen as sources of wisdom and guidance. They may possess knowledge of ancient traditions, folklore, and magical practices that they share with others, especially younger witches.

Bad Witch (Wicked Witch)

Malevolence: Bad witches are characterized by their malevolent intentions. They often use their magical powers for personal gain, revenge, or causing harm to others. Their actions are driven by negative emotions like jealousy, anger, or greed.

Dark Magic: Bad witches may engage in dark or forbidden magic, using curses, hexes, and black magic to bring misfortune and suffering to their targets. They may form alliances with dark entities or spirits.

Manipulation: Bad witches are skilled manipulators. They may use their magic to deceive or control others for their own purposes, often leading to negative consequences for those who fall under their influence.

Selfishness: Bad witches are often selfish and prioritize their own interests over others'. They may use their powers to accumulate wealth, power, or control at the expense of those around them.

Disregard for Nature: Bad witches may exploit or abuse nature and its elements for their own gain, causing ecological imbalance. They may engage in destructive rituals or practices.

Isolation: Bad witches may be isolated or feared by their communities due to their malevolent actions. They may live in solitude, away from society, to avoid detection or retaliation.

The distinction between "good" and "bad" witches is not as clear-cut, and individuals practicing modern witchcraft or Wicca, for example, often follow diverse belief systems and ethical guidelines that may not fit neatly into these categories.

Chapter Six

Witches in Literature: From Macbeth to Modern Novels

Witches have long been a fascinating and often complex presence in literature. They have appeared in various genres, from classic works of fiction to modern-day novels, and have captivated readers with their mystical powers, enigmatic personalities, and often ambiguous moralities. Here is an extensive description of witches in literature:

Mythology and Folklore

Witches have deep roots in mythology and folklore, where they often represent the intersection of magic and the human world. In ancient myths and legends, they are depicted as powerful beings with supernatural abilities, capable of both good and evil. Examples include the witch Circe from Greek mythology, who transformed Odysseus's crew into animals, and the sorceress Morgan le Fay from Arthurian legend.

Shakespearean Witches

William Shakespeare's plays have contributed significantly to the portrayal of witches in literature. In "Macbeth," the three witches, also known as the Weird

Sisters, play a pivotal role in manipulating Macbeth's fate and driving the tragic events of the play. Shakespeare's witches are often depicted as mysterious, otherworldly beings with the ability to foretell the future.

Fairy Tales

Witches frequently appear in fairy tales, often as antagonistic figures or sources of conflict for the protagonists. In stories like "Hansel and Gretel" and "Sleeping Beauty," witches use their magical powers to threaten or harm the main characters. These portrayals reflect cultural fears and cautionary messages about the dangers of encountering unknown forces.

Gothic Literature

In Gothic literature, witches often embody the dark and supernatural elements of the genre. They can be portrayed as eerie and malevolent figures, working in the shadows to manipulate events or exact revenge. The character of the mysterious witch in Nathaniel Hawthorne's "Young Goodman Brown" is an example of a witch who tempts the protagonist into delving into his darkest impulses.

Modern Fantasy Novels

In contemporary fantasy literature, witches are often multifaceted characters with complex motivations. They can be protagonists, anti-heroes, or formidable villains. Authors like Terry Pratchett ("Discworld" series), Ursula K. Le Guin ("Earthsea Cycle"), and J.K. Rowling ("Harry Potter" series) have created memorable and diverse witch characters who navigate worlds filled with magic, adventure, and moral dilemmas.

Feminist Literature

In feminist literature, witches are sometimes reimagined as symbols of feminine power and agency. These portrayals challenge traditional stereotypes and explore themes of female empowerment, self-discovery, and resistance against patriarchal systems. Examples include the witchy women in novels such as Alice

Hoffman's "Practical Magic" and Marion Zimmer Bradley's "The Mists of Avalon."

Magical Realism

Witches often make appearances in magical realism, blurring the lines between reality and fantasy. They exist in worlds where magic is an integral part of everyday life, and their presence can have profound effects on the characters and the narrative. Isabel Allende's "The House of the Spirits" and Gabriel Garcia Marquez's "One Hundred Years of Solitude" feature enchanting witches who shape the destinies of the characters.

Witches in literature embody a wide range of characteristics, from wise and benevolent figures to cunning and malevolent beings. They serve as symbols of power, rebellion, mystery, and transformation, and their portrayal in literature reflects cultural beliefs, fears, and aspirations. The depiction of witches in literature continues to evolve, offering readers an ever-expanding universe of magical and captivating characters.

Chapter Seven

The Covent of the Black Forest: Germany's 16th-Century Witches

The following three chapters are a bit more sensationalism while at the same time giving those interested in witchcraft an opportunity to reflect on past and present generalizations.

The dense, shadowy expanse of Germany's Black Forest has long been a place of mystery and folklore. Tales of spirits, dark magic, and hidden secrets abound in its depths, but one legend stands out among them all—the story of the Covent of the Black Forest. This 16th-century witches' coven was rumored to be a powerful and feared group, practicing ancient rituals that struck terror into the hearts of villagers. Accused of summoning spirits, brewing deadly potions, and controlling the forces of nature, the witches of the Black Forest left an indelible mark on history.

The Covent of the Black Forest was said to be composed of women—often healers and midwives—who lived on the fringes of society. In an era where female independence was often equated with witchcraft, these women were viewed with suspicion. The coven was rumored to have passed down ancient knowledge for generations, drawing from a blend of pagan traditions, herbal medicine, and early alchemical experiments. While some considered them wise women, others feared them as wielders of dark magic.

One of the most infamous figures linked to the coven was Frau Gertrude von Aichberg, a woman believed to be the high priestess of the group. She was said to possess an uncanny ability to foresee the future, heal the sick, and, if provoked, curse her enemies. Local legends describe how she and her followers gathered deep in the forest under the cover of darkness, performing rituals to harness the power of the elements.

The 16th century was a time of great superstition and religious fervor. With the Protestant Reformation sweeping across Europe and the Catholic Church tightening its grip, anything deemed unholy was met with swift and often violent retribution. Villagers began to whisper about strange occurrences linked to the coven: livestock falling dead overnight, sudden illnesses sweeping through communities, and eerie lights flickering deep within the forest.

Tensions escalated when a local nobleman, Baron Otto von Weidenfels, accused the coven of cursing his family. His eldest son had fallen into a mysterious fever, and his crops had withered despite the season being favorable. Desperate for an explanation, he turned to the growing hysteria surrounding witches and pointed the finger at Frau Gertrude and her followers.

This accusation ignited a chain reaction. In 1591, local authorities launched an investigation, led by Inquisitor Heinrich Waldemar, a notorious witch hunter. His methods were brutal, employing torture to extract confessions. Under duress, some villagers claimed they had seen the witches summon spirits or dance with the Devil himself. Others testified that the coven used enchanted powders to manipulate their enemies.

The hunt for the Black Forest witches reached its climax in late 1591. Several women suspected of being part of the coven were captured and imprisoned in the dungeons of Württemberg. Their trials were swift and cruel, with little chance for defense.

Among the accused was Frau Gertrude von Aichberg, whose trial became the most infamous of them all. Despite enduring extreme torture, she refused to confess to witchcraft. But the court, eager for a spectacle, sentenced her to death. On October 13, 1591, she and six other women were burned at the stake in the town square of Freiburg. Their executions were meant to serve as a warning to others, reinforcing the authority of both the Church and the ruling elite.

Although the Covent of the Black Forest was destroyed, whispers of its magic lived on. Some believed that a few members escaped into the depths of the forest, continuing their practices in secret. Over the centuries, stories persisted of ghostly apparitions in the Black Forest, unexplained lights flickering in the trees, and strange symbols appearing on ancient stones.

Today, the legend of the coven remains a fascinating part of German folklore. Historians debate whether the group truly existed as a powerful force of witches or if they were simply victims of mass hysteria. Regardless, their story serves as a reminder of the dangers of superstition, fear, and the brutal history of the European witch trials.

The Covent of the Black Forest is a tale of mystery, magic, and persecution. Whether these women were healers, cunning folk, or something more sinister will never be fully known. But their legend endures, woven into the fabric of one of Europe's most haunted landscapes. Even today, as travelers walk the winding paths of the Black Forest, some claim to feel an unseen presence, watching from the shadows—a reminder that the past is never truly gone.

Chapter Eight

The Mora Coven: Sweden's Infamous 17th-Century Witch Trials

The 17th century was a time of fear and superstition across Europe, and Sweden was no exception. One of the most infamous events in the country's history was the Mora Witch Trials, where accusations of witchcraft led to the execution of numerous individuals. At the heart of these trials was the so-called Mora Coven, a group of alleged witches said to have participated in dark rituals and supernatural acts. The hysteria surrounding this coven swept through Sweden, leaving a legacy of fear and tragedy.

Mora, a small town in central Sweden, became the epicenter of one of the largest witch hunts in Swedish history. The trials took place in 1669, during a period of intense religious fervor and growing paranoia about witchcraft. Reports of witches abducting children and taking them to the mythical Blåkulla—a legendary place where the devil held grand gatherings—spread like wildfire.

The idea of the Mora Coven emerged when children, pressured by authorities and religious leaders, began confessing that they had been taken to Blåkulla by their neighbors and family members. These supposed witches were accused of flying on broomsticks, attending demonic feasts, and making pacts with the devil himself. The sheer number of accusations led to widespread panic, with townspeople believing that an organized network of witches had infiltrated their community.

The Swedish authorities, influenced by a strong Lutheran faith and the belief that witchcraft was a real and present danger, launched a series of investigations into the suspected Mora witches. More than 300 people were accused of witchcraft, with many of them being children coerced into testifying against adults. The hysteria reached its peak when over 60 women were put on trial, with allegations based mostly on the testimony of young children.

One of the most chilling aspects of the Mora Witch Trials was the use of torture and public fear to extract confessions. Suspected witches were interrogated brutally, often subjected to sleep deprivation, beatings, and psychological manipulation. Those who confessed to witchcraft were sometimes spared execution but were still punished severely, while those who denied the charges often faced death by beheading or burning.

The Mora Coven was said to engage in a range of sinister activities, most notably their journeys to Blåkulla. According to the testimonies of children and other witnesses, these witches would use enchanted tools—such as broomsticks, animals, or even human skulls—to fly to their meetings.

At Blåkulla, they allegedly participated in feasts where they ate unnatural foods, danced with demons, and swore allegiance to the devil. Some children claimed that they were forced to attend these gatherings, where they were given gifts to ensure their loyalty to the dark forces. These tales, though clearly the result of mass hysteria and manipulation, were accepted as undeniable proof of the witches' guilt.

The Mora Witch Trials led to one of the largest mass executions in Sweden's history. In the fall of 1669, a total of 85 people were found guilty of witchcraft. Of these, 71 were sentenced to death, including 65 women, two men, and four boys. These individuals were executed by beheading, and their bodies were then burned to prevent any chance of resurrection through supernatural means.

The children who had testified against the witches were also punished, as Swedish authorities feared that they had been tainted by demonic influence. Many of them were beaten publicly and given religious education to cleanse them of their supposed involvement with the devil.

The Mora Witch Trials were part of a broader pattern of witch hunts that swept across Europe in the 16th and 17th centuries. Unlike in other countries, where witches were often burned at the stake, Sweden primarily used beheading as the preferred method of execution. Despite this difference, the sheer scale of the Mora executions marked a dark chapter in the nation's history.

Historians today recognize the trials as an example of mass hysteria, fueled by religious extremism, social tensions, and political motives. Many of those accused were likely innocent victims of fear and superstition, caught in a wave of paranoia that was difficult to escape.

By 1676, the Swedish government, realizing the extent of the wrongful executions, began questioning the validity of the witch hunts. The hysteria gradually faded, and King Charles XI implemented measures to prevent future mass executions based on unsubstantiated claims. The Mora Witch Trials remain one of the most infamous witch hunts in history, a cautionary tale of the dangers of fear-driven persecution.

The story of the Mora Coven is a chilling reminder of the power of mass hysteria and the consequences of blind faith in superstition. While modern society has largely moved beyond the fear of witches, the lessons from Mora continue to resonate. The trials stand as a symbol of the dangers of panic, misinformation, and the willingness to condemn others without proper evidence.

Today, Mora is known for its beautiful landscapes and cultural heritage, yet its history remains marked by the tragic events of 1669. The Mora Witch Trials serve as a stark warning against repeating the mistakes of the past, ensuring that such horrors remain confined to history rather than resurfacing in new forms of persecution and injustice.

Chapter Nine

The Coven of the Silver Moon

One of the most infamous modern covens that stirred controversy and fear in the past 50 years is the Coven of the Silver Moon in the United Kingdom. While not as widely known as some historical witch trials, this secretive group gained notoriety in the 1970s and 1980s for its alleged involvement in dark rituals, disappearances, and clashes with law enforcement.

The Coven of the Silver Moon was founded in the early 1970s in rural England, reportedly in Cornwall or Somerset, both areas with long-standing traditions of witchcraft and folklore. Unlike Wiccan groups focused on nature, healing, and positive spellwork, this coven was rumored to practice necromancy, blood magic, and ritualistic sacrifices. They claimed to harness the power of the moon for their workings, drawing inspiration from ancient pagan rites and medieval grimoires.

While many modern witches embrace an ethical approach to magic, the Silver Moon coven was feared for its dangerous and secretive nature. Witnesses and former members spoke of midnight ceremonies in the woods, where initiates were subjected to intense psychological rituals and oaths of absolute secrecy.

Mysterious Disappearances: Several individuals who were believed to be connected to the group vanished under strange circumstances. While no evidence directly linked the coven to foul play, rumors swirled that those who tried to leave met grim fates.

Animal Sacrifices: Reports emerged of ritually slaughtered animals being found near their alleged meeting sites, fueling fears of dark magic.

Threats Against Outsiders: Those who attempted to investigate the coven or expose its secrets often received threats, reinforcing the group's fearsome reputation.

By the 1980s, the Coven of the Silver Moon had become the subject of local legend and police scrutiny. Parents warned their children to stay away from certain wooded areas, and some locals claimed they saw shadowy figures conducting moonlit rituals. At the height of the Satanic Panic in the late 1980s, media outlets ran sensationalized stories about dangerous occult groups, and the coven was frequently mentioned in whispered speculation.

Authorities launched investigations but never found enough evidence to charge any individuals with crimes. Some researchers believe that elements of the coven went underground, while others insist it disbanded due to internal conflicts and fear of exposure.

By the early 1990s, the Coven of the Silver Moon seemingly faded into obscurity, though some believe that remnants of the group still exist today. Occult researchers and paranormal investigators claim to have traced former members to modern esoteric groups, but there has been no confirmed activity linked to the original coven in decades.

To this day, the legend of the Silver Moon coven lingers, with whispered stories of an underground network of witches who still gather in secret, practicing rites that mainstream witchcraft communities reject. Whether it was a case of hysteria, myth, or true occult danger remains one of the eerie mysteries of modern witchcraft history.

Chapter Ten

Witches in Pop Culture: Television, Film, and Fashion

Witches have had a significant presence in pop culture, captivating audiences through various mediums and genres. From movies and television shows to music and fashion, witches have become iconic and influential figures.

Movies

Witches have been a popular subject in film, both in classic and contemporary cinema. From "The Wizard of Oz" (1939) to "Hocus Pocus" (1993) and "Practical Magic" (1998), witches have been portrayed in unusual ways, ranging from wicked and malevolent to sympathetic and empowered characters. Movies like "The Craft" (1996) and "The Witches" (2020) have explored the complexities of witchcraft and the experiences of young women discovering their magical abilities.

Television Shows

Witches have been featured in numerous television shows, captivating audiences with their mystical powers and compelling storylines. "Bewitched" (1964-1972) is a classic sitcom that portrays a witch living among humans and trying to lead a normal life. "Charmed" (1998-2006) follows the lives of three sisters who discover they are powerful witches destined to protect innocents. Recent shows like "American Horror Story: Coven" (2013) and "Chilling Adventures of Sabrina" (2018-2020) have brought witches into the forefront of popular culture with darker and edgier narratives.

Music

Witches have also been a source of inspiration in music. Artists like Stevie Nicks and her band Fleetwood Mac have embraced witchy aesthetics and lyrical themes, adding an enchanting and mystical quality to their music. Songs like "Rhiannon" and "Seven Wonders" evoke the imagery and symbolism associated with witchcraft. Additionally, witchcraft and witchy elements have been incorporated into the aesthetics and performances of various musical genres, from rock and metal to pop and alternative.

Fashion and Style

The aesthetic of witches has influenced fashion and style trends, with witchy elements being incorporated into clothing, accessories, and makeup. Dark, flowing garments, mystical symbols, and occult-inspired jewelry have become trendy fashion choices. The witchy aesthetic often embraces a sense of individuality, empowerment, and mystique.

Literature and Comics

Witches have long been featured in literature and comic books, captivating readers with their magical abilities and complex personalities. Popular book series like "Harry Potter" by J.K. Rowling and "The Witcher" by Andrzej Sapkowski explore the world of witches and magic in rich detail. Comics like "Sabrina the Teenage Witch" and "The Sandman" have introduced memorable witch characters and delved into their magical adventures.

Video Games

Witches have also made their mark in the world of video games. Games like "The Witcher" series, "Dragon Age: Origins," and "Bayonetta" feature powerful witch characters as protagonists or key figures in the game's narrative. These games often incorporate elements of magic, spells, and witchcraft, allowing players to immerse themselves in fantastical worlds.

Social Media and Online Communities

The rise of social media platforms has created spaces where modern witches can connect, share their practices, and inspire others. Online communities, forums, and social media accounts dedicated to witchcraft have gained popularity, providing a platform for witches to discuss their beliefs, share rituals, and support each other in their spiritual journeys.

Witches in pop culture have become iconic and influential figures, representing empowerment, individuality, and a connection to the mystical and supernatural. They continue to captivate audiences across different mediums, shaping trends, and inspiring individuals to embrace their own magical potential. The portrayal of witches in pop culture reflects society's fascination with the mysterious and the desire for personal empowerment and self-expression.

Chapter Eleven

Witchcraft and Feminism: Empowerment and Identity

In this chapter, we will analyze the connection between witchcraft and feminism, focusing on the empowerment of women and the reclamation of feminine power.

Witchcraft and feminism have a complex and intertwined history that spans several decades. The connection between the two is rooted in the reclamation of feminine power, the empowerment of women, and the challenge of patriarchal systems. Here is an extensive description of the relationship between witchcraft and feminism:

Historical Perspective*:* In the context of the witch trials and persecution that occurred during the Early Modern period, women who were accused of witchcraft were often those who defied societal norms, challenged patriarchal authority, or possessed knowledge and skills outside the accepted boundaries. The association of witchcraft with women and the subsequent persecution of witches can be seen as a reflection of the deep-rooted fear and suppression of feminine power.

Reclamation of Feminine Power: In the feminist movement of the 20th century, there was a resurgence of interest in witchcraft as a means of reclaiming feminine power and spirituality. Many feminists saw parallels between the oppression of witches in the past and the ongoing marginalization and subjugation of women in society. Embracing witchcraft became a way to connect with ancient goddess traditions, reclaim women's spiritual autonomy, and challenge the patriarchal structures that perpetuated inequality.

Goddess Spirituality: Feminist witches often draw inspiration from goddess-based spiritual traditions that honor the divine feminine. They see the goddess as a symbol of feminine power, wisdom, and creativity. Embracing goddess spirituality allows women to explore their own divine nature and reclaim their inherent worth and value.

Witchcraft as Liberation: For many feminists, witchcraft represents a form of liberation and empowerment. It offers a framework for exploring and expressing personal power, intuition, and creativity. Witchcraft encourages individuals to trust their own instincts, develop their own spiritual practices, and challenge oppressive systems. It provides a space for self-discovery, healing, and personal transformation.

Intersectionality and Inclusivity: The modern feminist witchcraft movement strives for inclusivity and recognizes the intersectionality of identities and experiences. It acknowledges that witchcraft is not limited to one gender or one specific group of people. It embraces diversity and seeks to create a supportive and inclusive community where individuals from all backgrounds can find their place and contribute their unique perspectives.

Rituals of Empowerment: Feminist witches often incorporate feminist values and themes into their rituals. These rituals may focus on healing from patriarchal trauma, reclaiming body autonomy, honoring sisterhood, and solidarity, or celebrating the achievements and contributions of women throughout history. Rituals become spaces for personal empowerment, collective healing, and envisioning a more equitable and just future.

Activism and Social Justice: Many feminist witches see their practice as inseparable from activism and social justice work. They use their magical and spiritual practices to amplify their voices, support marginalized communities, challenge oppressive systems, and create positive change in the world. Witchcraft becomes a tool for both personal transformation and collective liberation.

Witchcraft and feminism can manifest in diverse ways. Not all witches identify as feminists, nor do all feminists practice witchcraft. However, the historical connections and the shared values of empowerment, equality, and challenging patriarchal norms have contributed to a significant overlap between these two movements.

Chapter Twelve

Witchcraft and Community Traditions

Witchcraft and folklore often thrive within close-knit communities, where knowledge and practices are shared among practitioners. These communities may have their own rituals, ceremonies, and celebrations that are specific to their beliefs and traditions. Folklore helps to reinforce a sense of identity, cultural heritage, and shared experiences within these communities.

Modern Witchcraft Revival: In the mid-20th century, there was a resurgence of interest in witchcraft, driven by movements such as Wicca and the broader neo-pagan movement. Influenced by ancient traditions, folklore, and ceremonial magic, these modern witchcraft practices embraced the worship of nature, goddess spirituality, and the honoring of ancestral wisdom. This revival helped reclaim the positive aspects of witchcraft and provided a platform for modern witches to connect and practice together.

Community and Traditions: The witch community today is incredibly diverse, encompassing various traditions, paths, and belief systems. Witches may follow specific traditions such as Wicca, Traditional Witchcraft, Hedge Witchcraft, Kitchen Witchcraft, or eclectic practices. Each tradition has its unique rituals, customs, and practices, but all share a reverence for nature, a connection to the divine, and the use of magic to manifest intentions.

The witch community fosters a sense of camaraderie and support among its members. Covens, circles, and online platforms provide spaces for witches to gather, share knowledge, and participate in group rituals. Festivals and gatherings, such as pagan and witchcraft conventions, offer opportunities for community building, workshops, and celebration of the seasons.

The modern witch community also embraces inclusivity and emphasizes the empowerment of individuals of all genders, sexual orientations, races, and backgrounds. Many witches are actively engaged in social justice, environmental activism, and promoting the principles of equality, diversity, and sustainability.

Personal Practice and Rituals: Within the witch community, personal practice and rituals play a vital role. Witches engage in meditation, divination, spell work, energy healing, and the study of magical correspondences. They work with various tools such as crystals, herbs, tarot cards, candles, and ritual implements, like wands and athames. Rituals are performed to honor deities, mark the turning of the seasons, celebrate life events, and work magic to manifest desires and intentions.

Overall, the witch community and tradition have evolved over time, reclaiming ancient wisdom, promoting empowerment, and fostering a sense of interconnectedness with nature and the spiritual realm. Through their practices and beliefs, witches seek personal growth, spiritual fulfillment, and the promotion of positive change in themselves and the world around them.

Evolution and Adaptation: Witchcraft and folklore have evolved over time, adapting to changing cultural, social, and religious contexts. They have absorbed influences from a diverse range of cultures, incorporating new elements and perspectives. In contemporary times, witchcraft has experienced a revival, with various modern practices, such as Wicca and neo-paganism, blending ancient traditions with contemporary spiritual beliefs.

Witchcraft and folklore are rich and diverse aspects of human culture, reflecting our fascination with the mystical, our connection to nature, and our desire to understand the unknown. They encompass a wide range of beliefs, practices, and stories that have shaped societies, preserved traditions, and inspired imagination throughout history. Exploring witchcraft and folklore provides insights into the human experience, our relationship with the supernatural, and the power of storytelling and community.

Chapter Thirteen

Witchcraft and Healing: Herbalism, Remedies, and Modern Practices

Witchcraft and healing have a long-standing relationship, as the practice of witchcraft often involves the use of various tools, rituals, and spells to promote physical, emotional, and spiritual well-being. Here is an extensive description of witchcraft and healing:

Holistic Approach

The relationship between a holistic approach to medicine and witches is characterized by a shared emphasis on treating the whole person, integrating mind, body, and spirit, and recognizing the interconnectedness of all aspects of health and well-being.

A holistic approach to medicine acknowledges that individuals are complex beings, and their health and wellness are influenced by multiple factors, including physical, emotional, mental, and spiritual dimensions. Rather than focusing solely on symptoms, holistic medicine seeks to understand and address the underlying causes of illness or imbalance within an individual.

Similarly, witches approach healing from a holistic perspective, recognizing that health is not just the absence of disease but a state of overall well-being and harmony. Witches often embrace a holistic worldview that views individuals as interconnected with nature and the universe. They understand that the health of the physical body is intertwined with emotional, mental, and spiritual aspects.

Witches often integrate various healing modalities and practices into their approach, drawing from ancient wisdom, folk traditions, and personal intuition. This may include herbal medicine, energy healing, rituals, spells, divination, meditation, and other techniques aimed at restoring balance, promoting self-awareness, and supporting the body's natural healing abilities.

The holistic approach and the witchcraft approach share a common belief in the power of the individual's innate healing abilities. Both approaches recognize that the body possesses inherent wisdom and the capacity to heal itself when provided with the necessary support and conditions. This view emphasizes the importance of empowering individuals to take an active role in their healing process, fostering self-care, and cultivating a deeper connection with their own bodies and intuition. They elieve that healing is more than a plastic bottle of pills.

Both approaches encourage preventive care and focus on maintaining optimal health and well-being. By addressing imbalances at their root causes and promoting lifestyle changes, such as nutrition, exercise, stress reduction, and emotional well-being, illnesses are prevented, and vitality is pushed to the forefront.

Although holistic medicine and witchcraft share similar principles and perspectives, they are not one and the same. Holistic medicine encompasses a wide range of practices and is recognized within conventional medical systems, while witchcraft is a spiritual and magical practice that may incorporate holistic principles into its approach to healing. Additionally, holistic medicine is grounded in scientific evidence and often works in conjunction with conventional medical treatments, whereas witchcraft may involve practices that are not scientifically validated.

Herbal Medicine

The relationship between witches and herbal medicine has deep historical roots. Throughout history, witches have been associated with the knowledge and use of herbs for both healing and magical purposes. In many traditional societies, witches were often the primary healers, utilizing their understanding of plants and their medicinal properties to provide remedies for various ailments.

Witches, for centuries, have possessed extensive knowledge of local plants, their properties, and their applications in healing. They would gather herbs from the wild or cultivate them in their own gardens, carefully selecting and preparing plant materials to create potions, salves, and teas for medicinal use.

Herbal medicine played a significant role in the practices of witches, as they believed in the inherent healing power of nature. They recognized that plants contained potent substances that could support the body's natural healing processes and promote well-being. Witches understood the importance of using the right plants in the right dosage and combination to address specific ailments. They were the predecessors for modern day homeopathy.

Additionally, witches often incorporated magical and spiritual elements into their herbal medicine practices. They believed that certain plants possessed not only physical healing properties but also metaphysical qualities that could be harnessed for spiritual purposes. They would perform rituals, spells, and incantations while working with herbs to enhance their healing effects or to address underlying energetic imbalances.

Furthermore, the practice of herbal medicine was closely tied to the cycles of nature and the seasons. Witches would align their healing practices with lunar phases, planetary influences, and other natural rhythms. They believed that working in harmony with nature's cycles would amplify the potency of their herbal remedies.

The association between witches and herbal medicine has often been misunderstood or misrepresented throughout history. In many cases, societal fears and prejudices led to the persecution and demonization of witches and their practices. This resulted in a negative portrayal of both witches and herbal medicine, often labeling them as "witchcraft" or "folk magic" and associating them with malevolence or dark forces.

However, in contemporary times, there has been a revival and reclamation of the knowledge and practices of witches and herbal medicine. Many modern witches, herbalists, and holistic healers draw inspiration from the wisdom of traditional witches and their use of herbs for healing. They combine ancient knowledge with scientific understanding to create safe and effective herbal remedies for various health conditions.

Energy Healing

Energy healing refers to various practices that involve the manipulation and balancing of subtle energy within the body to promote physical, emotional, and spiritual well-being.

From the eras of King David and Nordic Gods, witches have been associated with the manipulation and understanding of energy. They believed in the existence of a universal life force or energy that permeates all things, often referred to as mana, chi, prana, or vital force. Witches were believed to possess the ability to tap into and direct this energy for healing purposes.

In many traditional societies, witches utilized various techniques to work with energy. These techniques often included laying on of hands, energy channeling, aura cleansing, and ritual practices. Witches would identify energetic imbalances or blockages within individuals and use their knowledge and intuition to facilitate the flow of energy, promoting healing and restoring balance.

In contemporary times, the relationship between witches and energy healing has evolved. Many modern witches incorporate energy healing practices into their spiritual and magical work. They draw from a range of modalities, including Reiki, chakra balancing, crystal healing, and other energy-based approaches, to facilitate healing on physical, emotional, and energetic levels.

For witches, energy healing is often seen as a complementary practice that aligns with their understanding of the interconnectedness of all things and the power of intention and focused energy. They may combine energy healing techniques with other magical practices, such as spellcasting, divination, or ritual, to enhance the energetic effects and promote holistic healing.

While witches may engage in energy healing, not all energy healers identify as witches. Energy healing is a diverse field with practitioners from various backgrounds and belief systems. The association between witches and energy healing should not be generalized or assumed for all energy healers.

Furthermore, it is essential to approach the topic of witches and energy healing with an open mind and respect for individual beliefs and practices. The contemporary witchcraft community encompasses a wide range of perspectives and approaches, and not all witches engage in energy healing or vice versa.

In conclusion, the relationship between witches and energy healing is rooted in historical beliefs and practices. Witches have long been associated with the manipulation and understanding of energy for healing purposes. In modern times, many witches incorporate energy healing techniques into their spiritual and magical work, recognizing the power of energy to promote healing and balance. However, it's important to acknowledge the diversity within both the energy healing and witchcraft communities and approach the topic with an open and nuanced perspective.

Rituals and Spells

Rituals and spells are fundamental practices within witchcraft, serving as powerful tools for witches to manifest their intentions, connect with spiritual forces, and create desired outcomes.

Rituals can be seen as structured and intentional ceremonies or actions performed by witches to create a sacred space, honor deities or spirits, and invoke specific energies. These rituals often involve a combination of symbolic gestures, spoken words, offerings, and the use of various tools such as candles, crystals, herbs, and incense. Witches may perform rituals during specific lunar phases, seasonal festivals, or significant life events to mark transitions, seek guidance, or engage in spiritual communion.

Spells, on the other hand, are specific actions or incantations performed with the intention of manifesting a desired outcome or change. Spells can be seen as focused rituals, utilizing the manipulation of energy, symbolism, and personal will to bring about transformation. Witches may use spoken words, written symbols, visualizations, or physical objects to cast spells. The spells can be aimed at healing, protection, love, abundance, or any other intention depending on the witch's goals and needs.

Witches believe in the power of intention and the ability to influence the energetic and spiritual realms through rituals and spells. They often work with correspondences, such as planetary influences, moon phases, elemental associations, and the properties of herbs, crystals, and colors, to enhance the potency and alignment of their rituals and spells. Witches draw upon their knowledge of symbolism, folklore, and magical traditions to create meaningful and effective rituals and spells.

The practice of rituals and spells within witchcraft is deeply personal and can vary widely among individuals and traditions. Witches may follow established rituals and spellcasting techniques passed down through generations, or they may create their own unique practices based on their intuition, individual experiences, and spiritual beliefs. There is no one-size-fits-all approach, and witches often adapt and evolve their rituals and spells as they deepen their understanding and connection with their craft.

To summarize, rituals and spells are central components of witchcraft, allowing witches to tap into their personal power, connect with the spiritual realm, and manifest their intentions. These practices are deeply rooted in symbolism, energy manipulation, and spiritual beliefs. The relationship between witches, rituals, and spells is one of profound symbiosis, enabling witches to channel their intentions and create meaningful change in their lives and the world around them.

Divination and Intuition

Divination is the practice of seeking knowledge or insight about the past, present, or future through various methods, such as tarot cards, runes, astrology, scrying, or other symbolic systems. It is a means for witches to tap into higher guidance, connect with spiritual energies, and gain deeper understanding or foresight. Divination tools are used as channels or focal points to access intuitive information and receive messages from the unseen realms.

Witches often incorporate divination into their spiritual and magical practices to seek guidance, make informed decisions, and navigate life's challenges. Divination allows them to explore outcomes, understand underlying energies, and gain insight into the situations they encounter. By interpreting symbols, patterns, or messages revealed through divination, witches can uncover hidden knowledge or uncover potential paths for personal growth, healing, or manifestation.

Intuition, on the other hand, is an inherent and intuitive knowing or inner guidance that comes from within. It is the ability to perceive or understand something instinctively, without the need for conscious reasoning. Intuition is considered a powerful tool for witches, as it allows them to access their inner wisdom, connect with their higher selves, and navigate the realms of magic and spirituality.

Witches cultivate and trust their intuition, viewing it as a valuable resource for making decisions, interpreting signs, and sensing energies. They may develop practices such as meditation, grounding, or energy work to enhance their intuitive abilities. By honing their intuitive skills, witches can attune themselves to subtle energies, read the energetic vibrations of people or situations, and receive guidance from their own higher consciousness or spiritual allies.

In the practice of witchcraft, divination and intuition often go hand in hand. Divination tools serve as external aids to access intuitive information, while intuition acts as the internal compass that guides the interpretation and application of the divinatory messages received. Witches rely on their intuitive insights and instincts to understand the deeper meanings and messages embedded within divination readings.

Ancestral Healing

Ancestral healing is a practice that involves connecting with and honoring one's ancestors for the purpose of healing and personal growth. It is based on the belief that our ancestral lineage carries both blessings and burdens that can influence our lives. By acknowledging, understanding, and working with our ancestral lineage, witches seek to heal ancestral wounds, resolve generational patterns, and cultivate a sense of wholeness and empowerment.

Ancestral healing acknowledges that our ancestors, both blood-related and chosen, exist beyond the physical realm and continue to have a presence and influence in our lives. It recognizes that ancestral energy and wisdom can be accessed for guidance, healing, and support. Witches often engage in practices that foster a deep connection with their ancestors, such as ancestor altars, rituals, prayers, or meditation.

The practice of ancestral healing involves several key aspects:

1. Acknowledgment and Gratitude: Witches recognize and express gratitude for their ancestral lineage, honoring the contributions and sacrifices made by their ancestors. They acknowledge that they are part of a larger web of lineage and inherit both the strengths and challenges of their ancestors.

2. Healing Ancestral Wounds: Ancestral healing involves addressing and healing unresolved wounds and traumas within the ancestral lineage. Witches may engage in rituals, energy work, or guided meditations to release and transmute ancestral pain, fostering healing not only for themselves but also for past and future generations.

3. Ancestral Connection and Guidance: Witches seek to establish a conscious and ongoing relationship with their ancestors. They may communicate with their ancestors through prayer, meditation, or divination practices to receive guidance, wisdom, and support in their own lives.

4. Rituals and Ceremonies: Witches often incorporate rituals and ceremonies specifically focused on ancestral healing. These may include creating ancestor altars, offering libations or gifts, performing rituals during ancestral holidays or significant dates, or participating in ances-

tral healing circles or group ceremonies.

5. Inheriting and Honoring Gifts: Witches believe that they inherit gifts, talents, and wisdom from their ancestors. They explore and embrace these inherited qualities, honoring the ancestral lineage by using their gifts to bring healing and positive change to themselves and their communities.

Ancestral healing is deeply personal and can vary among individuals and traditions. Each witch may develop their own rituals, practices, and methods based on their intuitive connection and ancestral lineage. The practice often emphasizes respect, reverence, and the intention to foster healing, growth, and alignment with the wisdom of the past.

Understand that ancestral healing is not about idealizing or romanticizing the past, but rather about understanding and working with the complexities of our ancestral lineage. It may involve confronting difficult aspects of our ancestry and engaging in the process of forgiveness, healing, and transformation.

Spiritual Connection

Spiritual connection and healing encompass a deep and profound relationship between individuals and their spiritual essence, higher power, and/or the divine. It involves recognizing and nurturing the inherent spiritual aspect of one's being (soul) and tapping into its transformative power to promote healing and well-being on various levels.

Spiritual connection is the process of developing a conscious relationship with the spiritual dimensions of existence. It involves cultivating a sense of interconnectedness, meaning, and purpose beyond the physical realm. This connection can be experienced through various practices such as prayer, meditation, contemplation, or engagement in rituals and ceremonies.

Through spiritual connection, individuals can experience a sense of unity, transcendence, and profound inner peace. It offers a pathway to accessing higher wisdom, guidance, and insight. By developing a regular spiritual practice, individuals can deepen their connection with their inner selves, the natural world, and the spiritual forces that surround them.

Spiritual healing is the process of restoring balance, harmony, and wholeness on a spiritual, emotional, mental, or physical level. It acknowledges that imbalances or disease can manifest when there is a disruption or disharmony in the spiritual aspects of a person's being. Spiritual healing seeks to address these imbalances by reconnecting individuals with their spiritual essence and facilitating the flow of divine energy.

Spiritual healing can take various forms, depending on the individual's beliefs, practices, and cultural background. It may involve energy healing, such as Reiki or other modalities that work with subtle energies, to promote balance and remove energetic blockages. It may also incorporate practices like prayer, visualization, or affirmation to invoke divine assistance and activate the innate healing capacity within. Furthermore, spiritual healing recognizes the interconnectedness of mind, body, and spirit. It acknowledges that emotional and mental well-being are closely intertwined with spiritual well-being. By addressing the spiritual aspects of an individual's being, spiritual healing can support and enhance the healing process on other levels.

Spiritual healing often encompasses personal growth, self-discovery, and transformation. It encourages individuals to explore their core beliefs, values, and purpose in life, and to align their actions and choices with their highest spiritual values. It can facilitate the release of past traumas, limiting beliefs, or negative patterns, allowing individuals to step into their authentic selves and live more fulfilling and purposeful lives.

Spiritual connection and healing are deeply personal and subjective experiences. Everyone may have their own unique understanding of spirituality and may approach spiritual practices and healing in separate ways. It's crucial to respect and honor diverse spiritual paths and belief systems, as spiritual connection and healing can be expressed and experienced in countless ways.

Emotional and Shadow Work: The relationship between emotional and shadow work is integral to a witch's process of healing and personal growth. Both forms of inner exploration and self-reflection are essential for understanding and integrating the various aspects of our psyche, bringing about deep healing and transformation.

Emotional work involves acknowledging, understanding, and processing our emotions in a healthy and constructive manner. It involves cultivating emotional intelligence, becoming aware of our feelings, and developing the capacity to express and regulate them effectively. Emotional work encourages individuals to explore their emotional patterns, triggers, and wounds, with the goal of fostering emotional well-being and authenticity.

Shadow work focuses on the exploration and integration of the unconscious or repressed aspects of our psyche known as the "shadow." The shadow comprises the parts of ourselves that we have pushed away, denied, or disowned due to societal conditioning, shame, or fear. Shadow work entails bringing these aspects into conscious awareness, accepting them with compassion, and integrating them into our sense of self.

The relationship between emotional and shadow work can be described as follows:
    1. Identification of Emotional Triggers: Emotional work helps us identify and understand our emotional triggers and patterns. By becoming aware

of how we react emotionally to certain situations, we can delve deeper into the underlying beliefs, wounds, or unresolved issues that contribute to our emotional responses.

2. Uncovering the Shadow: Shadow work involves exploring the hidden or suppressed aspects of ourselves that have been repressed or disowned. These aspects often hold intense emotions, unresolved traumas, or unexpressed desires. Engaging in shadow work allows us to shed light on these hidden parts and bring them into conscious awareness.

3. Healing Emotional Wounds: Emotional work and shadow work go hand in hand in the healing process. By acknowledging and working through our emotional wounds, we can uncover the root causes that contribute to our emotional patterns. Shadow work helps us delve into the deeper layers of our psyche to understand the origins of these wounds, including any shadow aspects that may be influencing our emotional experiences.

4. Integration and Wholeness: Both emotional and shadow work aim to integrate and heal fragmented aspects of ourselves. Emotional work supports the expression, understanding, and acceptance of our emotions, fostering emotional wholeness. Shadow work allows us to embrace and integrate the disowned or suppressed parts of ourselves, fostering a sense of internal unity and wholeness.

5. Transformation and Personal Growth: The combined practice of emotional and shadow work can lead to profound personal growth and transformation. By exploring our emotions and shadow aspects, we gain insight into our patterns, beliefs, and behaviors. This self-awareness enables us to make conscious choices, heal past wounds, and develop healthier ways of relating to ourselves and others.

Emotional healing and shadow work can be intense and challenging, as they involve facing aspects of ourselves that we may have avoided or denied. *It is recommended to approach this work with support from therapists, coaches, or experienced practitioners who can provide guidance and create a safe space for exploration*

Witchcraft and healing intertwine to provide a comprehensive and empowering approach to well-being. Witches embrace nature's wisdom, harness their intuition, and utilize various practices and tools to facilitate healing on multiple levels. By acknowledging the mind-body-spirit connection and working with the natural energies of the world, witches empower individuals to take an active role in their own healing and to find balance, vitality, and wholeness.

Chapter Fourteen

Witchcraft and Shamanism: Exploring Altered States and Journeys

Witchcraft and shamanism share some common elements and can intersect in numerous ways. The following describes the relationship between witchcraft and shamanism:

Spiritual Practices: Both witchcraft and shamanism involve spiritual practices that connect practitioners with the spiritual realm and tap into unseen forces. Both paths involve working with energy, spirits, and altered states of consciousness to effect change, seek guidance, and promote healing.

Magic and Ritual: Witchcraft and shamanism often involve the use of magic and ritual to influence the spiritual and physical realms. Witches and shamans may perform spells, ceremonies, and rituals to harness and direct energy, commune with spirits, and manifest their intentions.

Connection with Nature: Both witchcraft and shamanism emphasize a deep connection with nature and recognize the inherent wisdom and power found in the natural world. Nature serves as a source of inspiration, healing, and spiritual guidance for practitioners of both paths. Witches and shamans may work closely with plants, animals, and natural elements to access their energies and incorporate them into their spiritual practices.

Journeying and Spirit Work: Shamanism places a strong emphasis on shamanic journeying, which involves entering altered states of consciousness to travel to the spirit realm and communicate with spirit guides, power animals, and ancestral spirits. Witches may also engage in journeying and spirit work to connect with spirit allies, seek wisdom, and receive guidance from the spiritual realm.

Healing and Energy Work: Both witchcraft and shamanism involve practices related to healing and energy work. Shamans are known for their healing abilities and may use various techniques such as energy clearing, soul retrieval, and herbal medicine. Witches may also practice energy healing, create herbal remedies, or work with energy manipulation and manipulation of subtle energies for healing purposes.

Ancestral Connections: Shamanism often places importance on ancestral connections and seeks guidance and wisdom from ancestors. Witches, too, may honor and work with their ancestors, seeking their guidance and support in their spiritual practice. Ancestral connections are seen as a source of strength, wisdom, and ancestral knowledge.

Ritual Tools and Artifacts: Both witchcraft and shamanism utilize specific tools and artifacts in their practice. These may include items such as ritual drums, rattles, wands, crystals, and divination tools. These objects hold symbolic and energetic significance and are used to facilitate rituals, communicate with spirits, and channel energy.

Community and Solo Practice: Both witchcraft and shamanism can be practiced individually or within community settings. Some practitioners work within specific traditions and lineages, while others follow their own intuitive path. Community gatherings and ceremonies provide opportunities for shared experiences, learning, and support, while individual practice allows for personal exploration and connection with the spiritual realm.

While there are similarities between witchcraft and shamanism, they are distinct practices with their own unique histories, cultural contexts, and belief systems. Some individuals may incorporate elements of both paths into their spiritual practice, while others may focus primarily on one.

Chapter Fifteen

Witchcraft and Ethics: Moral Codes and Responsible Magick

Witchcraft, like any other spiritual or religious path, encompasses various ethical principles and guidelines that practitioners may adhere to. While individual beliefs and interpretations may vary, there are common themes and values that are often associated with witchcraft ethics.

Harm None: The "Harm None" principle, also known as the Wiccan Rede, is a central ethical guideline in many forms of witchcraft. It promotes the idea of avoiding intentional harm to others, including oneself, and encourages practitioners to act responsibly and with compassion.

Personal Responsibility: Witchcraft emphasizes personal responsibility and accountability for one's actions and intentions. Practitioners are encouraged to be mindful of the consequences of their words, actions, and magical workings and to take responsibility for the outcomes they create.

Respect for Free Will: Witchcraft upholds the importance of respecting the free will and autonomy of others. Practitioners are encouraged to seek consent and permission before conducting any magical work that may impact others and to refrain from interfering with the choices and decisions of others.

Balance and Harmony: Many witches strive to maintain balance and harmony in their lives and in the world around them. This involves recognizing and honoring the interconnectedness of all things and working to restore balance and harmony when it is disrupted.

Environmental Stewardship: Witchcraft often emphasizes a deep reverence for nature and encourages practitioners to be mindful of their impact on the environment. This includes practicing sustainable living, supporting conservation efforts, and working to restore and protect the natural world.

Honesty and Integrity: Witchcraft values honesty and integrity in all aspects of life. Practitioners are encouraged to be truthful in their words and actions, to act with integrity, and to cultivate authenticity in their spiritual practice.

Self-Reflection and Growth: Witchcraft encourages self-reflection and personal growth as an ongoing process. Practitioners are encouraged to examine their beliefs, attitudes, and behaviors, and to continually strive for personal and spiritual development.

Non-Discrimination and Inclusivity: Many witches embrace principles of non-discrimination and inclusivity, recognizing and honoring the diversity of individuals and communities. This involves rejecting prejudice and discrimination based on factors such as race, gender, sexual orientation, or religious beliefs.

Ethical Spell craft: In spell craft, witches are encouraged to consider the ethical implications of their intentions and to ensure that their magical workings align with their ethical principles. This includes avoiding spells that manipulate or control others without their consent and focusing on positive intentions that promote healing, growth, and well-being.

Witchcraft is a diverse and evolving practice, and ethical beliefs and practices can differ from different traditions or individual practitioners. Each witch has their own personal code of ethics that they follow based on their own moral compass, spiritual beliefs, and understanding of the craft. It is essential for witches to engage in ongoing self-reflection, study, and dialogue with others to develop and refine their ethical framework within the practice of witchcraft.

Chapter Sixteen

Witchcraft and Nature Spirituality

Witchcraft and nature spirituality are deeply interconnected, as witchcraft often emphasizes the reverence for and connection with the natural world. The following describes the relationship between Witchcraft and nature spirituality.

Sacredness of Nature: In witchcraft, nature is seen as inherently sacred and imbued with divine energy. Witches view the natural world as a source of wisdom, inspiration, and spiritual power. They recognize the interconnectedness of all living beings and the importance of living in harmony with nature.

Wheel of the Year: Many witches follow the Wheel of the Year, which is a cycle of seasonal festivals that celebrate the changes in nature throughout the year. These festivals, also known as Sabbats, mark important moments such as the solstices, equinoxes, and agricultural milestones. By observing and honoring these cycles, witches attune themselves to the rhythms of nature and align their spiritual practice with the natural world.

Elemental Energies: Witches often work with the energies of the four classical elements: Earth, Air, Fire, and Water. These elements represent several aspects of nature and symbolize different qualities and energies. Witches may call upon these elemental energies in rituals, spells, and meditations to invoke specific qualities or to harmonize with the natural forces around them.

Nature-Based Rituals: Witchcraft often involves the performance of rituals and ceremonies in natural settings. Witches may conduct rituals in forests, gardens, or other outdoor spaces to connect with the energies of the land, trees, plants, and animals. These rituals may involve offerings, invocations, meditation, and spellcasting, all with the intention of attuning to nature and seeking its guidance and blessings.

Herbalism and Plant Magic: Witches have a deep relationship with plants and herbs, viewing them as allies for healing, magical work, and spiritual connection. Herbalism plays a significant role in witchcraft, with witches utilizing the properties and energies of various plants for medicinal purposes, spell work, and ritual practices. Witches may create herbal remedies, potions, or use dried herbs in rituals and spell craft.

Animal Connections: Witches often forge connections with animals and recognize their spiritual significance. Animal symbolism is used in divination, as messengers from the spiritual realm, and as sources of guidance and protection. Witches may work with animal totems or incorporate animal imagery into their rituals and magical practices to honor the wisdom and energy of the animal kingdom.

Nature Spirits and Deities: Witchcraft acknowledges the presence of nature spirits, such as fairies, elves, and spirits of the land. These spirits are believed to inhabit and protect natural spaces and can be invoked or honored in rituals. Additionally, witches may honor deities associated with nature and fertility, such as goddesses and gods of the earth, harvest, or wildlife.

Nature-based Divination: Nature itself can be a source of divination for witches. They may engage in practices such as reading signs and omens from natural occurrences, using elements of nature for scrying (e.g., water, crystals, or mirrors), or employing natural objects like stones, shells, or bones for divinatory purposes. By connecting with the natural world, witches seek insights and guidance from the greater web of life.

Witchcraft and nature spirituality intertwine to create a profound appreciation for the Earth, its cycles, and its creatures. The practice of witchcraft emphasizes living in harmony with nature, finding spiritual connection through natural elements, and working in partnership with the energies present in the natural world. Through this connection, witches seek to cultivate a deep reverence for nature, access its transformative energies, and align themselves with the rhythms and wisdom of the Earth.

Chapter Seventeen

Witchcraft and Mediumship: Communicating with the Spirit World

Mediumship, as a practice of communication with the spirit world, has a rich history that predates the modern witchcraft movement. While mediumship is not exclusive to witchcraft, it has been incorporated into various magical and spiritual traditions, including some forms of witchcraft. The following describes mediumship in witchcraft, as well as a brief overview of its history and origins:

Mediumship in Witchcraft: Mediumship in witchcraft refers to the practice of communicating with spirits, ancestors, deities, or other entities from the spiritual realm. It involves a medium, a person with the ability to connect with and receive messages from the spirit world. In the context of witchcraft, mediums may use their abilities to seek guidance, receive messages, or perform divination for themselves or others. Mediumship in witchcraft can involve various methods such as channeling, trance work, spirit possession, or connecting with spirits through tools like divination tools or ritualistic practices.

History and Origins of Mediumship

The practice of mediumship can be traced back to ancient civilizations and spiritual traditions throughout the world. Here are some notable historical and cultural examples:

Ancient Greece and Rome: In ancient Greece and Rome, spiritual practices involved oracles and priestesses who acted as mediums, delivering messages from the gods. The Oracle of Delphi in Greece and the Sybil of Cumae in Rome are famous examples of ancient mediums.

Spiritualism Movement: In the 19th century, the Spiritualism movement gained popularity, particularly in Europe and the United States. Spiritualists believed in the ability to communicate with the spirits of the deceased, and mediums played a central role in conducting seances and relaying messages from the spirit world.

Shamanic Traditions: Shamanic practices found in various cultures involve spirit communication through trance, journeying, and possession. Shamans act as intermediaries between the human world and the spirit realm, often performing healing and divinatory functions.

Indigenous Spiritual Practices: Many indigenous cultures have long-standing traditions of spirit communication. Indigenous shamans, medicine people, and spiritual leaders often serve as mediums, communicating with ancestral spirits, nature spirits, and deities for guidance and healing purposes.

Folklore and Witchcraft: Within the realm of folklore and witchcraft, mediums and spirit communication have been prevalent throughout history. Folk healers, wise women, and cunning folk would often use their abilities to communicate with spirits for divination, healing, and protection.

Mediumship has evolved and diversified over time, with diverse cultures and spiritual traditions incorporating their unique practices and beliefs. In contemporary witchcraft, mediumship continues to be embraced by some practitioners as a means of connecting with the spiritual realm, seeking guidance, and deepening their spiritual practice.

Chapter Eighteen

Witchcraft and Modern Spirituality: An Evolving Path

Witchcraft and modern spirituality intersect in many ways as witches and individuals seek to explore their spiritual beliefs, connect with nature, and reclaim ancient wisdom in contemporary contexts. The following is an informative page devoted to witchcraft and modern spirituality.

Nature-Based Spirituality: Witchcraft often embraces a nature-based spirituality, recognizing the interconnectedness of all living beings and the inherent wisdom found in the natural world. Modern practitioners of witchcraft draw inspiration from indigenous and ancient traditions that revered nature and its cycles, incorporating rituals, ceremonies, and practices that honor and align with the natural elements.

Personal Empowerment: Modern witchcraft emphasizes personal empowerment and self-discovery. Practitioners seek to reclaim their own power, intuition, and agency, rather than relying on external authorities. Witchcraft encourages individuals to explore their own spiritual path, develop their magical skills, and connect with their inner wisdom and authenticity.

"Magick" and Intention: Modern witchcraft often incorporates the practice of magick, which involves harnessing natural and spiritual energies to manifest intentions and desires. Through spells, rituals, and other forms of magical work, practitioners focus their energy and intention to create positive change in their lives and the world around them.

Ritual and Ceremony: Rituals and ceremonies play an integral role in modern witchcraft. These practices help create sacred space, honor deity or spiritual entities, mark significant life events, and connect with the divine. Rituals often involve the use of symbols, candles, herbs, crystals, and other tools to facilitate spiritual connection and transformation.

Ancestor Reverence: Many modern witches place importance on ancestral reverence and lineage. They seek to connect with their ancestral roots, honor their ancestors' wisdom, and integrate ancestral practices and rituals into their spiritual path. Ancestor veneration allows for a deeper understanding of personal and cultural heritage and fosters a sense of connection with the past.

Eclectic and Personalized Approach: Modern witchcraft embraces an eclectic and personalized approach to spirituality. Practitioners are encouraged to explore and synthesize diverse spiritual beliefs, practices, and traditions that resonate with them. This allows for a flexible and adaptable spiritual path that reflects individual needs, interests, and experiences.

Community and Collaboration: Modern witchcraft often emphasizes the importance of community and collaboration. Practitioners come together in covens, circles, or online communities to share knowledge, support one another's spiritual growth, and engage in collective rituals and celebrations. Collaboration and sharing of wisdom enhance the richness and depth of the spiritual experience.

Ethical Framework: Many modern witches follow ethical guidelines that promote harmlessness, personal responsibility, and respect for others and the Earth. The Wiccan Rede, for example, encapsulates the principle of "Do what you will, harm none," emphasizing the importance of ethical decision-making and considering the consequences of one's actions.

Embracing Diversity and Inclusivity: Modern witchcraft strives to be inclusive and welcoming to individuals of all backgrounds, genders, sexual orientations, and cultural heritages. There is an increasing recognition of the importance of diversity and the need to challenge systems of oppression within spiritual communities.

Integration of Modern Tools and Technologies: Modern witches often incorporate modern tools and technologies into their practice. This includes using social media platforms, online resources, and digital apps to connect with like-minded individuals, access information, and share their spiritual experiences.

Witchcraft and modern spirituality provide a framework for individuals to explore their own beliefs, connect with the natural world, and cultivate personal empowerment. This intersection offers a diverse and evolving spiritual path that honors ancient wisdom while embracing contemporary perspectives and practices.

Chapter Nineteen

Witchcraft and Sexuality: Unraveling the Mystical and Sensual

Witchcraft and sexuality have an intertwined history, with practitioners often exploring and embracing sexuality as a sacred and empowering aspect of their spiritual path. Here is an extensive description of witchcraft and sexuality:

Sacred Sexuality: Within witchcraft, sexuality is often viewed as a sacred and natural expression of human experience. It is seen as a potent force for creativity, pleasure, and spiritual connection. Some practitioners engage in rituals and practices that incorporate sexual energy to enhance their magical workings and deepen their spiritual connection.

Body Positivity: Witchcraft promotes body positivity and self-acceptance, celebrating the diversity of bodies and challenging societal norms and beauty standards. Practitioners are encouraged to embrace their bodies, honor their physical desires, and cultivate a healthy and positive relationship with their sexuality.

Erotic Witchcraft: Erotic witchcraft explores the intersection of sexuality and magic, integrating sexual energy and desire into spell work, rituals, and personal empowerment practices. It involves tapping into the sensual and sexual aspects of one's being to fuel magical intentions and manifestation.

Sex Magic: Sex magic is a practice within witchcraft where sexual energy is harnessed and directed to manifest desires and intentions. It involves engaging in sexual acts or focusing on sexual arousal while holding a specific intention or visualizing a desired outcome. Sex magic can be practiced individually or with a consenting partner(s).

Goddess and Divine Feminine: Many witchcraft traditions honor and celebrate the divine feminine, including goddesses associated with love, sensuality, and fertility. The exploration of sexuality within witchcraft often involves invoking and connecting with these feminine energies to embrace and embody their empowering qualities.

LGBTQ+ Inclusivity: Witchcraft often embraces and celebrates diverse sexual orientations and gender identities. It provides a safe and inclusive space for LGBTQ+ individuals to explore and express their sexuality without judgment or discrimination. Witchcraft communities often emphasize acceptance, equality, and support for all sexual orientations and gender expressions.

Healing Sexual Trauma: Witchcraft can be a healing path for individuals who have experienced sexual trauma. Through rituals, energy work, and self-care practices, witchcraft provides tools for reclaiming personal power, healing wounds, and cultivating a healthy and positive relationship with one's sexuality.

Consent and Boundaries: Witchcraft emphasizes the importance of consent, boundaries, and ethical practices in all aspects of life, including sexuality. Practitioners are encouraged to engage in consensual and respectful sexual experiences, honoring the autonomy and agency of all individuals involved.

Sexual Education and Empowerment: Within witchcraft communities, there is often an emphasis on sexual education and empowerment. Practitioners may engage in discussions, workshops, or teachings that explore topics such as consent, healthy relationships, sexual pleasure, and reproductive health.

Embracing the Shadow: Witchcraft acknowledges the shadow aspects of human sexuality, including exploring and integrating the darker or taboo aspects of desire and pleasure. It encourages practitioners to embrace and understand their own sexual shadows as part of their holistic spiritual journey.

In the context of witchcraft, the term "sexual shadows" refers to the exploration and integration of the darker or taboo aspects of sexuality within an individual's spiritual journey. It involves acknowledging and working with the less conventional or socially accepted aspects of desire, pleasure, and sexual expression. Read below for a description of sexual shadows within the realm of witchcraft:

Taboo Desires: Sexual shadows encompass desires that may be considered unconventional, taboo, or outside societal norms. This can include exploring fantasies, fetishes, or practices that are not commonly discussed or accepted in mainstream culture.

Shadow Work: Within witchcraft, shadow work is a process of delving into the deeper layers of the psyche to uncover and integrate aspects of the self that have been repressed, denied, or deemed unacceptable. When it comes to sexual shadows, shadow work involves examining and embracing the hidden or repressed desires, thoughts, or experiences that may have been shamed or suppressed.

Healing Sexual Wounds: Sexual shadows can also pertain to unresolved or traumatic experiences related to sexuality. Engaging with sexual shadows allows individuals to confront and heal from past traumas, release shame or guilt, and reclaim their personal power and agency in their sexual expression.

Challenging Social Conditioning: Sexual shadows invite individuals to question and challenge societal conditioning and expectations around sexuality. It involves examining the cultural and social influences that may have shaped one's beliefs, attitudes, and behaviors regarding sex, and exploring alternative perspectives and practices.

Integration and Acceptance: Working with sexual shadows within witchcraft involves integrating these aspects into one's identity and spiritual practice. It is about accepting and embracing the full spectrum of one's desires and experiences, without judgment or self-censorship.

Sacred Transformation: Embracing sexual shadows in witchcraft can be seen as a sacred act of transformation and self-discovery. It allows individuals to explore and harness the transformative power of their sexual energy, promoting personal growth, empowerment, and a deeper connection to their own authentic desires.

Consent and Boundaries: When working with sexual shadows, it is crucial to maintain strong boundaries and prioritize consent. It is important to ensure that any exploration or experimentation is consensual, respectful, and safe for all parties involved.

Personal and Spiritual Growth: Engaging with sexual shadows within witchcraft offers the opportunity for personal and spiritual growth. It encourages individuals to embrace their whole selves, confront limiting beliefs or societal conditioning, and foster a deeper understanding and acceptance of their own unique sexual expression.

The exploration of sexuality within witchcraft is a personal and diverse experience, and practitioners are encouraged to honor their own boundaries, values, and comfort levels when incorporating sexuality into their spiritual path. Consent, respect, and personal empowerment are foundational principles in the intersection of witchcraft and sexuality.

Chapter Twenty

Familiars and Spirit Animals: Allies in the Witch's Craft

Familiars and spirit animals are integral concepts in witchcraft and spiritual practices. They are often seen as companions, guides, and sources of wisdom and support.

Familiars: Familiars are believed to be supernatural entities or spirits that form a spiritual bond with a witch or practitioner. They are often portrayed as animals, although they can also take the form of other creatures or even inanimate objects. Familiars are thought to assist witches in their magical workings, providing guidance, protection, and enhancing their powers.

Spiritual Companions: Familiars are seen as loyal and trusted companions on the witch's spiritual journey. They are believed to share a deep connection with the witch, understanding their thoughts, emotions, and intentions. Familiars are said to offer comfort, companionship, and a sense of spiritual kinship.

Power Enhancement: Familiars are thought to possess their own magical abilities and energies. When a witch works with their familiar, it is believed to amplify their own power and energy, enhancing their spell work, divination, and spiritual practices. Familiars are seen as conduits of magical energy, facilitating the witch's connection with the spiritual realm.

Symbolic Meanings: Familiars often carry symbolic meanings associated with the specific animal or creature they represent. These meanings can vary across cultural and spiritual traditions. For example, a black cat familiar may be associated with mystery, intuition, and psychic abilities, while a raven familiar may symbolize transformation, wisdom, and communication with the spirit world.

Spirit Animals: Spirit animals are like familiars but are not exclusive to witchcraft. They are believed to be spiritual guides and allies that offer support, wisdom, and protection. Spirit animals can appear in dreams, meditative states, or through signs and synchronicities in the physical world. They often embody certain qualities or characteristics that resonate with the individual, providing guidance and inspiration.

Animal Symbolism: Spirit animals are associated with specific qualities and attributes, reflecting their symbolic meaning in various cultures and spiritual practices. For example, the wolf may represent loyalty, intuition, and instinct, while the owl may symbolize wisdom, intuition, and the ability to see beyond illusions. Different animals are believed to bring specific messages and lessons to the individual.

Connection to Nature: Both familiars and spirit animals highlight the importance of connecting with nature and the animal kingdom. They remind us of our interconnectedness with the natural world and the wisdom that can be gained by observing and learning from animals. By forging a bond with a familiar or working with a spirit animal, individuals can deepen their connection to nature and tap into its transformative energies.

Personal Guidance: Familiars and spirit animals provide personal guidance and insight tailored to the individual's needs. They may appear during times of transition, challenges, or significant life events to offer support, wisdom, and reassurance. By working with these spiritual allies, individuals can access their inner wisdom, develop a stronger intuition, and navigate their spiritual path with confidence.

The understanding and interpretation of familiars and spirit animals can vary among different spiritual traditions and individual beliefs. Some may view them as literal entities, while others see them as symbolic representations or aspects of the individual's psyche. Regardless, familiars and spirit animals hold a special place in witchcraft and spiritual practices, providing companionship, guidance, and a deeper connection to the spiritual realm and the natural world

Chapter Twenty-One

The Coven: Bonds, Roles, and Traditions

A coven is a close-knit community of individuals who come together to practice witchcraft, magic, and spiritual rituals. The word "coven" typically refers to a group within Wicca or other pagan traditions, although it can also be used more broadly to describe any gathering of witches or practitioners of magic.

Covens often serve as a supportive and nurturing space where members can explore and deepen their understanding of their spiritual path. They provide a sense of belonging and camaraderie, as members share a common set of beliefs and practices. Within a coven, individuals can learn from one another, exchange knowledge and experiences, and support each other's growth and development as witches or practitioners.

Coven dynamics vary depending on the specific tradition, structure, and preferences of its members. Some covens are led by a High Priestess or High Priest, while others operate on a more egalitarian or democratic model. Roles and responsibilities may be assigned within the coven, such as the casting of circles, leading rituals, or teaching specific areas of magical practice.

Covens typically meet regularly, often during specific lunar phases, seasonal celebrations (such as Sabbats), or other significant dates in accordance with their spiritual tradition. Rituals, spell work, divination, meditation, and study are commonly practiced within the coven setting. These gatherings provide opportunities for members to connect with the divine, work magic collectively, and strengthen their spiritual bond.

The formation of a coven involves trust, mutual respect, and often a shared vision or set of values. Covens may have specific criteria or requirements for accepting new members, such as a period of probation or initiation rituals to ensure compatibility and commitment. The size of a coven can vary, ranging from a handful of individuals to larger groups.

While covens offer a supportive and structured environment, they also come with responsibilities and expectations. Members are encouraged to contribute actively, participate in group activities, and uphold the values and ethics of their tradition. This includes maintaining confidentiality, honoring personal boundaries, and working towards personal growth and spiritual evolution.

Joining a coven can provide a rich and transformative experience for individuals seeking to deepen their magical practice, connect with a spiritual community, and explore the mysteries of the craft. However, it's important to find a coven that aligns with your beliefs, values, and goals. Each coven has its own unique energy, practices, and focus, so it's essential to do research, ask questions, and find the right fit for your personal journey.

To find a coven, you can consider the following options:

Local Pagan or Witchcraft Communities: Look for local pagan or witchcraft communities in your area. Attend pagan or Wiccan events, workshops, or festivals where you can connect with like-minded individuals who may be part of or have information about covens.

Online Pagan and Witchcraft Forums: Join online forums, discussion boards, or social media groups dedicated to paganism, witchcraft, or Wicca. Engage with the community, ask questions, and inquire if there are any active covens in your region.

Metaphysical or Occult Stores: Visit metaphysical or occult stores in your area. They may have notice boards or information about local covens or groups that you can join.

Seek Recommendations: Talk to individuals who are already practicing witchcraft or paganism. They might be able to recommend or connect you with a coven that aligns with your interests and beliefs.

It's important to note that not all covens are open to new members, as they may have specific requirements, traditions, or be invite-only. Respect their privacy and boundaries, and if you encounter rejection, continue exploring other avenues or consider starting your own practice as a solitary practitioner.

Chapter Twenty-Two

Modern Witchcraft Movements: Eclectic Practices and New Traditions

Modern witchcraft movements encompass a diverse range of practices and beliefs that have emerged and evolved in recent times.

Wicca

Wicca is one of the most well-known modern witchcraft movements. Gerald Gardner popularized the movement in the mid-20th century by drawing inspiration from ancient pagan and witchcraft traditions. Wicca emphasizes reverence for nature, the worship of a Goddess and God, the celebration of seasonal festivals (known as Sabbats), and the practice of magic and ritual. Wiccans often follow ethical guidelines such as the Wiccan Rede, which promotes the principle of "harm none."

Eclectic Witchcraft

Eclectic witchcraft is a flexible and individualized approach that incorporates elements from various traditions, practices, and belief systems. Eclectic witches often create their own unique blend of rituals, spells, and magical techniques based on their personal preferences and experiences. They may draw inspiration from Wicca, folk magic, ceremonial magic, and other occult traditions.

Kitchen Witchcraft

Kitchen witchcraft centers around the use of everyday household items and the preparation of food as a form of magic. Kitchen witches often incorporate herbs, spices, and other ingredients into their magical practices, such as creating herbal remedies, infusing intentions into meals, or brewing potions and teas. They view the kitchen as a sacred space for nurturing and healing.

Green Witchcraft

Green witchcraft focuses on working closely with nature and the natural world. Green witches have a deep connection to plants, herbs, and the environment, and often incorporate herbalism, gardening, and nature-based rituals into their practice. They may engage in activities such as herbal medicine, nature walks, plant-based spell work, and conservation efforts.

Traditional Witchcraft

Traditional witchcraft refers to various pre-modern witchcraft practices that have been revived and reconstructed. It draws inspiration from historical witchcraft folklore, folk magic, and regional witchcraft traditions. Traditional witches often emphasize ancestral connections, working with spirits and deities, and the use of traditional tools and rituals.

Chaos Magic

Chaos magic is a modern occult practice that emphasizes the belief that belief itself is a powerful tool in magic. Practitioners of chaos magic often employ a flexible and experimental approach, incorporating elements from diverse magical systems, symbols, and techniques. They may work with sigils, visualization, and ritual improvisation to manifest their intentions.

Feminist Witchcraft

Feminist witchcraft blends feminist ideology with witchcraft practices, highlighting the empowerment of women and the reclamation of feminine power. Feminist witches often focus on themes of gender equality, reclaiming women's spiritual history, and honoring the divine feminine. They may incorporate goddess worship, feminist rituals, and activism into their practice.

Modern Shamanism

Modern shamanism draws inspiration from traditional indigenous shamanic practices and adapts them to contemporary contexts. Modern shamans often engage in practices such as journeying, connecting with spirit guides and power animals, and performing energy healing. They may incorporate elements of drumming, chanting, and trance work to facilitate spiritual journeys and healing.

These are just a few examples of the diverse range of modern witchcraft movements. Each movement has its own unique practices, beliefs, and emphasis, reflecting the evolving nature of witchcraft in the modern era. Modern witchcraft movements provide individuals with the opportunity to explore their spirituality, connect with the natural world, and engage in magical practices that resonate with their personal beliefs and experiences.

Chapter Twenty-Three

Witches, Religion, and Christianity: Intersections and Conflicts

Yes, witches can be Christians. When discussing witches and religion, it is imperative to understand that that witchcraft is not inherently tied to a specific religion. While some practitioners of witchcraft may follow pagan or Wiccan beliefs, there are also individuals who identify as witches and incorporate their practices into their Christian faith.

In some cases, Christian witches may view their craft as a form of spiritual expression and connection with the divine. They may integrate elements of witchcraft, such as ritual work, spell craft, or divination, into their Christian worship and personal spirituality. These individuals often emphasize the use of their craft for healing, guidance, and positive transformation, while maintaining a deep devotion to their Christian beliefs and values.

Christian witches who practice witchcraft often interpret biblical passages, stories, and symbols in ways that align with their understanding of magic, nature, and personal empowerment. They may draw inspiration from biblical figures associated with magic or mysticism, such as Moses or King Solomon.

It is important to recognize that the term "witch" can have different meanings and connotations depending on the cultural and historical context. In some Christian denominations, "witch" may be associated with negative stereotypes and associations with Satanism or evil. However, it is essential to approach the topic with an open mind and respect for diverse spiritual practices and beliefs.

The compatibility of witchcraft and Christianity is a matter of personal interpretation and individual faith. Just as there are various interpretations of Christianity itself, there is diversity within the witchcraft community. Some Christians may view witchcraft as incompatible with their beliefs, while others may find ways to incorporate both aspects into their spiritual journey.

Witches and Religion

Witches and religion have a complex and varied relationship that spans cultures, time periods, and belief systems. The concept of witches and their association with religion has evolved throughout history, leading to different interpretations and understandings. Enjoy the following on witches and religion:

Historical Perspectives:

Witches, in the popular imagination, are often associated with witchcraft, which is traditionally seen as a practice that involves supernatural powers and the manipulation of magical forces. In many ancient and indigenous cultures, witchcraft was an integral part of religious and spiritual practices. These traditions recognized the existence of individuals who possessed special knowledge and abilities to commune with spirits, manipulate energies, or serve as intermediaries between the earthly realm and the divine.

Religious Persecution:

However, with the rise of Christianity and the spread of monotheistic religions, the perception of witches and witchcraft underwent a significant transformation. In many cases, witches were demonized and seen as threats to religious orthodoxy and societal order. The association between witches and religion became deeply intertwined with accusations of heresy, devil worship, and malevolent practices.

During periods such as the European witch hunts and the Salem Witch Trials, witches were persecuted and subjected to harsh punishments, often based on religious beliefs and fears. These historical events contributed to the negative stigma and fear associated with witches, particularly in Christian-dominated societies.

Contemporary Interpretations:

In modern times, the understanding of witches and their relationship with religion has become more diverse and nuanced. There are various spiritual and religious paths that incorporate witchcraft or magical practices, such as Wicca, Paganism, and various forms of modern witchcraft. These paths often embrace a reverence for nature, the cycles of the seasons, and a connection to the divine or the sacred.

For many modern witches, their practices are deeply spiritual and can be viewed as a form of religious expression. Some witches may identify as Wiccans, who follow a nature-based spirituality that honors the divine in both masculine and feminine aspects. Others may align with specific pagan traditions, such as Celtic, Norse, or indigenous spiritualities, which incorporate magical practices within their religious frameworks.

Recognize that not all witches identify as adherents of a particular religious tradition. Some may practice witchcraft as a personal spiritual path that is separate from organized religion. They may draw upon eclectic influences, personal beliefs, or a combination of spiritual practices to shape their craft.

It is crucial to understand that witchcraft and religion are not monolithic concepts. There are countless interpretations and practices within the witchcraft community, each influenced by individual beliefs, cultural backgrounds, and firsthand experiences. Some witches may incorporate elements of Christianity, Judaism, or other established religions into their craft, blending magical practices with their religious faith.

The relationship between witches and religion is a complex and multifaceted topic. It varies depending on historical, cultural, and personal contexts. As with any religious or spiritual path, it is important to approach the subject with an open mind, respect for diversity, and a willingness to learn from different perspectives.

Chapter Twenty-Four

Spirit Work and Spirit Communication: Reaching Beyond the Veil

Witches and spirit work or spirit communication have a deep-rooted connection, as witches often seek to communicate with spirits, guides, ancestors, and other spiritual entities as part of their practice. The paragraphs below are just a brief synopsis and each category is catalogued in more detail in other chapters.

Understanding Spirit Work:

Spirit work, also known as spirit communication or spirit connection, is the practice of establishing a connection with spirits and working with them for various purposes. It involves communicating, receiving messages, seeking guidance, and even forming alliances with spirits. Spirit work can be done through various methods, including meditation, divination, trance, ritual, and mediumship.

Witches and Spirit Work:

Witches have long been known for their ability to communicate with spirits and engage in spirit work. They recognize and honor the existence of spirits, seeing them as integral parts of the natural and spiritual realms. Witches often view spirits as allies, teachers, and sources of wisdom and support. They may seek guidance from ancestral spirits, work with elemental spirits, or establish relationships with deities and spirit guides.

Methods of Spirit Communication:

Witches employ various techniques and tools for spirit communication, depending on their personal preferences and the tradition they follow. Some common methods include:

Divination: Witches may use divination tools like tarot cards, runes, pendulums, or scrying mirrors to receive messages and insights from the spirit realm.

Ritual and Ceremony: Rituals and ceremonies are performed to create sacred space and invite spirits to communicate. These may involve the use of candles, incense, offerings, and specific invocations or prayers.

Meditation and Trance: Witches practice meditation and trance techniques to enter altered states of consciousness, allowing for easier connection with spirits. This can involve visualization, breathing exercises, and deep relaxation.

Mediumship: Some witches possess natural mediumistic abilities and can directly communicate with spirits, acting as intermediaries between the physical and spiritual realms.

Dreamwork: Dreams provide a gateway for spirit communication. Witches may engage in dream rituals, lucid dreaming, or keep dream journals to receive messages from the spirit realm.

Ethics and Safety in Spirit Work:

Witches approach spirit work with a keen sense of ethics and responsibility. They emphasize consent, protection, and establishing clear boundaries when working with spirits. Witches often develop personal codes of conduct to ensure respectful and ethical interaction with the spirit realm. They may use protective rituals, grounding techniques, and spiritual hygiene practices to safeguard themselves during spirit work.

Spirit Work for Healing and Growth:

Witches engage in spirit work not only for seeking guidance but also for personal healing and growth. They may work with spirits to release negative energies, gain spiritual insight, or receive healing on an emotional, physical, or energetic level. Through spirit work, witches aim to deepen their spiritual connection, expand their knowledge, and cultivate personal empowerment

Spirit work requires dedication, knowledge, and discernment. Witches approach spirit work with respect, humility, and a commitment to personal growth and ethical practice. They understand the complexities of the spirit realm and strive to maintain balanced and harmonious relationships with the spirits they encounter.

Chapter Twenty-Five

Symbols and Rituals in Witchcraft: Tools and Traditions

I should mention that this is the longest chapter in the book, so dig in, get yourself comfortable.

Symbols and rituals are integral components of both witchcraft and folklore. They serve as tools for communication, spiritual connection, and the manifestation of magical intent. Common symbols associated with witchcraft include pentagrams, moon phases, herbs, crystals, and various ritual objects. Rituals can involve spellcasting, invocation of deities or spirits, use of divination tools, and the performance of specific gestures or actions believed to have mystical significance.

Witch symbols and rituals play a significant role in the practice of witchcraft. Here is an extensive description of some commonly used symbols and rituals:

Symbols:

Pentacle/Pentagram: The pentacle, also known as the pentagram, is a symbol with a long and diverse history. It is a five-pointed star that is enclosed within a circle. The word "pentacle" is often used to refer specifically to a pentagram inscribed within a disc or a flat, two-dimensional object, whereas "pentagram" denotes the five-pointed star itself.

The pentacle/pentagram has been used and interpreted by various cultures and belief systems throughout history. Its origins can be traced back to ancient civilizations, including Mesopotamia, Egypt, and Greece. In these cultures, the pentagram held different meanings and was associated with different deities and concepts.

In ancient Mesopotamia, the pentagram was associated with the Sumerian goddess Inanna and later with the Babylonian goddess Ishtar. It symbolized divine protection, the five elements (earth, air, fire, water, and spirit), and the power of the goddess.

In ancient Egypt, the pentagram represented the concept of "microcosm," symbolizing the human body with its five extremities (head, two arms, and two legs). It was also linked to the goddess Isis and her protective and healing qualities.

In ancient Greece, the pentagram held multiple meanings. It was associated with the Pythagorean philosophy, where each point represented one of the five elements and embodied principles such as health, beauty, and wisdom. The pentagram was also linked to the goddess Venus, symbolizing love and femininity.

The pentacle/pentagram has also played a significant role in various religious and spiritual traditions. In Wicca and modern Paganism, the pentagram is a sacred symbol representing the five elements (earth, air, fire, water, and spirit) and the connection between them. It is often used in rituals and ceremonies, and it can be seen as a symbol of protection, balance, and unity.

In occultism and esoteric traditions, the pentacle/pentagram has been associated with magic, ritual practices, and the summoning of spirits. It has been used as a symbol of personal power and spiritual transformation.

The meaning and interpretation of the pentacle/pentagram have varied throughout history and continue to do so today. Its significance is often shaped by the context in which it is used and the beliefs and intentions of the individual or group employing it.

It is worth noting that the pentacle/pentagram has also been associated with negative connotations in certain contexts. In Christian demonology, for example, the inverted pentagram is sometimes linked to satanic or malevolent symbolism. However, it is essential to recognize that such associations are not inherent to the symbol itself but rather arise from specific cultural or religious beliefs.

Overall, the pentacle/pentagram remains a powerful and versatile symbol with rich historical and symbolic significance. Its diverse interpretations reflect the wide range of human beliefs, values, and spiritual practices throughout the ages.

Moon: The moon holds a significant role as a symbol and source of inspiration in witchcraft. Its cycles and phases are closely observed and utilized in various rituals and magical practices. The moon's energy is believed to influence the ebb and flow of magic, emotions, and spiritual energies.

In witchcraft, the moon is often associated with the divine feminine, intuition, and the subconscious mind. It represents the cyclical nature of life, renewal, and transformation. The moon is seen as a source of guidance, illumination, and hidden knowledge.

The lunar phases play a crucial role in magical workings. The most recognized phases are the New Moon, Waxing Moon, Full Moon, and Waning Moon.

New Moon: The New Moon symbolizes new beginnings, fresh starts, and setting intentions. It is a time for planting seeds, initiating projects, and envisioning goals. Witches often perform rituals focused on manifestation, setting intentions, and divination during this phase.

Waxing Moon: As the moon begins to grow in size, it is referred to as the Waxing Moon. This phase represents growth, abundance, and attraction. It is a time for increasing energy, taking action, and amplifying intentions. Spells related to manifestation, growth, and prosperity are commonly performed during this phase.

Full Moon: The Full Moon is a time of heightened energy, illumination, and power. It symbolizes completion, fruition, and the climax of magical energy. Many witches consider this phase as the most potent for spell work, divination, and charging tools and crystals. Rituals for healing, intuition, and manifestation are frequently conducted during the Full Moon.

Waning Moon: As the moon begins to decrease in size, it is known as the Waning Moon. This phase represents release, banishing, and letting go. Witches often work with the Waning Moon to remove obstacles, break negative patterns, and release what no longer serves them. Banishing spells, cleansing rituals, and cord-cutting ceremonies are common during this phase.

Beyond the lunar phases, different moon names are used to identify specific energies associated with certain months or events. For example, the Blue Moon refers to a second Full Moon within the same calendar month and is considered a time of heightened magic and potent energy.

In addition to working with lunar phases, witches may also align their magical practices with specific moon signs or astrological correspondences. Each zodiac sign is associated with different energies and qualities, and incorporating this knowledge can enhance the effectiveness of rituals and spell work.

Moon-related tools, such as Moonwater (water charged under the moonlight), moonstone crystals, and moon-themed artwork, are often used in witchcraft to channel lunar energy and create a connection with the moon's symbolism.

Ultimately, the moon in witchcraft represents a deep connection to nature, intuition, and the spiritual realm. Its phases, energy, and symbolism offer witches a powerful framework for working magic, setting intentions, and harnessing the cyclical energies of the universe

Triple Moon/Goddess: The Triple Moon, also known as the Triple Goddess symbol, is a well-known and widely recognized emblem in witchcraft and pagan spirituality. It represents the three phases of the moon—waxing, full, and waning—and is associated with the Triple Goddess archetype.

The Triple Goddess represents the various aspects of the divine feminine and the cycles of life, death, and rebirth. Each phase of the moon corresponds to a specific aspect of the Goddess:

Waxing Crescent: The Waxing Crescent phase represents the Maiden aspect of the Goddess. It symbolizes youth, new beginnings, growth, and potential. The Maiden is associated with independence, curiosity, exploration, and the fresh energy of spring. She embodies the qualities of innocence, enthusiasm, and new ventures.

Full Moon: The Full Moon phase represents the Mother aspect of the Goddess. It symbolizes abundance, fertility, nurturing, and fulfillment. The Mother is associated with creation, nurturing, protection, and the abundant energy of summer. She embodies the qualities of compassion, love, and caretaking.

Waning Crescent: The Waning Crescent phase represents the Crone aspect of the Goddess. It symbolizes wisdom, introspection, transformation, and letting go. The Crone is associated with endings, release, wisdom, and the reflective energy of autumn and winter. She embodies the qualities of experience, knowledge, and spiritual guidance.

Together, the three phases of the Triple Moon symbolize the complete cycle of life and the continuous journey of growth, transformation, and renewal. It represents the interconnectedness and interdependence of these three aspects of the feminine divine.

The Triple Moon symbol is often used in rituals, spells, and magical tools. It can be found on altar cloths, jewelry, candles, and various other objects. Witches and pagans may incorporate the symbol into their practices to honor the divine feminine, invoke the energies of the Goddess, and connect with the cycles of nature.

It is important to note that the Triple Moon/Goddess symbol has its roots in ancient mythology and pagan traditions, particularly in relation to lunar and earth-based religions. However, its interpretation and usage may vary among individuals and different pagan paths. Some may emphasize the specific attributes and qualities of each aspect of the Goddess, while others may view the symbol as a representation of the overall unity and wholeness of the divine feminine.

Overall, the Triple Moon/Goddess symbol serves as a powerful reminder of the cyclical nature of life, the divine feminine, and the interconnectedness of all things. It holds deep meaning for those who embrace the Goddess as a source of inspiration, wisdom, and spiritual connection in their spiritual practices.

Broomstick:

The broomstick holds a fascinating history and symbolism in the context of witchcraft and magical folklore. While it is commonly associated with witches and flying, its significance goes beyond mere transportation. Historically, the broomstick has been linked to various cultural practices and beliefs, dating back centuries. It is important to note that the association between broomsticks and witchcraft is rooted in folklore and myth rather than historical reality.

One theory suggests that the broomstick's connection to witches stems from ancient fertility rituals. In agricultural societies, brooms were sometimes used in rituals to symbolize sweeping away negative energies or to invoke good luck and bountiful harvests. Over time, these rituals became intertwined with the concept of witches and their ability to harness natural energies for magic.

The notion of witches flying on broomsticks emerged during the time of the European witch trials in the 16th and 17th centuries. It was believed that witches, often depicted as women, would apply a special ointment to their bodies that contained hallucinogenic herbs. They would then use a broomstick or a similar tool to apply the ointment to their genitals. This process was thought to facilitate astral projection or hallucinatory experiences, leading to the belief that witches could fly on broomsticks.

It is worth mentioning that these beliefs were primarily based on superstitious fears and societal anxieties surrounding witchcraft during that period. Actual historical evidence of witches flying on broomsticks is nonexistent.

In magical practice today, the broomstick carries symbolic significance rather than being used as a means of transportation. It is seen as a tool of transformation, purification, and protection. The broomstick is often associated with the element of air and is used in rituals to sweep away negative energies, cleanse a space, or create a boundary between the mundane world and the magical realm.

Witches may incorporate broomsticks into their rituals by "sweeping" or "energetically cleansing" an area before performing spells or divination. This act is symbolic of clearing away stagnant energy and preparing the space for magical work.

In addition to its ritualistic use, the broomstick is also seen as a symbol of female power and independence. The broomstick's association with women and witchcraft challenges traditional gender roles and societal expectations, empowering individuals to embrace their own magical abilities and inner strength.

While the broomstick has become an enduring symbol of witchcraft and magical practice, it is essential to approach its history and symbolism with an understanding of its mythological roots and cultural context. The broomstick's role in witchcraft extends beyond its popularized image, embodying the themes of transformation, purification, and personal empowerment.

Cauldron

The cauldron is a potent and iconic symbol in witchcraft, steeped in rich symbolism, folklore, and magical associations. It holds a prominent place in both historical and contemporary magical practices, representing transformation, healing, and the mystical depths of the craft.

The cauldron's association with magic can be traced back to ancient times. It is often linked to the Celtic and Norse traditions, where cauldrons were considered sacred vessels with mystical properties. In Celtic mythology, the cauldron of the goddess Cerridwen was believed to possess the power of inspiration, transformation, and rebirth. It was a vessel of wisdom and contained a potent brew that granted knowledge and poetic inspiration.

In witchcraft, the cauldron serves as a symbol of the womb of the Earth, the cauldron of creation and rebirth. It represents the divine feminine energy and the cosmic womb of the goddess. The cauldron is associated with the element of water, which symbolizes emotions, intuition, and the subconscious mind.

The cauldron is used in various magical rituals and practices:

- Brewing and Potions: The cauldron is often used for brewing herbal concoctions, creating potions, and mixing magical ingredients. It serves as a vessel for combining different herbs, oils, and liquids to infuse them with magical intent and create transformative elixirs.

- Divination: The cauldron can be used as a scrying tool for divination. By filling the cauldron with water or other scrying mediums, witches can gaze into its depths to seek insights, visions, and messages from the spirit realm.

- Ritual and Spell work: The cauldron is frequently employed as a focal point for rituals and spellcasting. It is used to contain and amplify energy, serving as a sacred space for transformative magic. The cauldron can be used for burning herbs, incense, or candles, symbolizing the alchemical transformation of energies.

- Healing and Transformation: The cauldron is associated with the transformative powers of healing and personal growth. It represents the process of inner transformation and emotional healing, allowing individuals to delve into their subconscious, release what no longer serves them, and embrace positive change.

The cauldron's symbolism also extends to the concept of the Three Witches or the Triple Goddess, representing the three aspects of the divine feminine—the

Maiden, Mother, and Crone. The cauldron embodies the powers of creation, nurturing, and wisdom.

In addition to its symbolic and magical associations, the cauldron has a prominent place in folklore and mythology. It is often depicted in tales of witches and magic, such as the story of Macbeth by William Shakespeare, where the Three Witches stir their cauldron to conjure spells and prophecies.

Overall, the cauldron in witchcraft represents the sacred vessel of transformation, magic, and feminine power. It embodies the mysteries of creation, healing, and the hidden depths of the craft. Through its use in rituals, potions, and spellcasting, the cauldron serves as a powerful tool for witches to tap into their intuitive and magical abilities and connect with the realms of the divine.

Athame

The athame is a ceremonial knife or dagger that holds a significant role in witchcraft and occult practices. It is a tool commonly associated with rituals, energy manipulation, and the casting of circles. The athame's purpose is not for physical cutting or harming, but rather for directing and focusing magical energy.

The word "athame" is believed to have its origins in the Greek word "arthame," meaning "a sharp-edged weapon." The athame is often associated with the element of fire, representing the transformative power of will and intention.

The athame typically has a double-edged blade, although some variations may have a single-edged blade. The blade is often crafted from steel, but it can also be made from other materials such as iron or even wood, depending on personal preference and tradition. The handle is commonly made from wood, bone, or other natural materials and may be adorned with symbols or inscriptions. The athame holds several purposes and uses in witchcraft:

- Ritual Symbolism: The athame represents the masculine energy within witchcraft, balancing the feminine energy symbolized by the chalice. It is often seen as a phallic symbol, embodying strength, focus, and the power of manifestation.

- Casting and Opening Circles: The athame is utilized in the ritual of casting circles. A circle acts as a sacred and protected space for magical work. The witch will typically use the athame to trace the circumference of the circle, invoking the energies and establishing a boundary between the mundane and the magical realms.

- Directing Energy: The athame is employed to direct and manipulate magical energy during rituals and spell work. It serves as a conduit for the practitioner's intent, allowing them to focus and project their energy effectively. The blade can be used to draw symbols or sigils in the air, directing energy towards a specific purpose or goal.

- Invoking and Banishing: The athame is used in the invoking and banishing of energies or entities. It can be employed to call upon specific deities, elemental forces, or spirits, as well as to banish negative energies or unwanted influences.

- Symbolic Representation: The athame often holds personal symbolism for the witch. It may be consecrated and imbued with personal energy, making it a unique and powerful tool for ritual and magical practices.

It is worth noting that the athame is a tool of sacred importance and is typically handled with care and respect. It is commonly used solely by the witch who consecrated it, and it is not intended for mundane or everyday use.

The specific practices and symbolism associated with the athame can vary among different traditions and individuals. Some witches may choose to keep their athame strictly for ritual use, while others may incorporate it into their daily magical practices. Overall, the athame serves as a symbolic tool for directing and focusing energy within witchcraft.

Herbs and Plants

Herbs and plants hold a central role in witchcraft, serving as powerful symbols and tools for rituals, spells, and healing practices. The use of herbs and plants in witchcraft can be traced back to ancient times when people believed in the magical and medicinal properties of the natural world.

Symbolism: Each herb and plant carries its own unique symbolism, often based on its physical characteristics, historical associations, or mythological connections. For example, lavender is commonly associated with peace, relaxation, and purification, while rosemary is often linked to protection, clarity, and memory. The symbolic meanings assigned to herbs and plants can vary across different cultures and traditions.

Magical Properties: In addition to symbolism, herbs and plants are believed to possess specific magical properties and energies. These properties can be categorized into various categories, such as protective, purifying, love-enhancing, or healing. Witches often select herbs and plants based on their magical correspondences to align with their intentions and enhance the effectiveness of spells and rituals.

Correspondences: Herbs and plants are associated with different elements, planets, zodiac signs, and deities, creating a system of correspondences that witches utilize in their practices. For instance, sage is often connected with the element of air and the planet Jupiter, making it suitable for rituals related to wisdom, purification, and spiritual growth. These correspondences help witches align their intentions with the energies of the natural world.

Ritual and Spell work: Herbs and plants are integral components in a wide range of magical practices. They are used in various forms, including dried leaves, flowers, roots, essential oils, or herbal infusions. Witches may burn herbs as incense, create herbal sachets or charms, brew herbal teas, or use them in bath rituals and spell jars. Different methods of preparation and utilization allow witches to harness the specific properties and energies of herbs and plants.

Divination and Herbalism: Herbs and plants are utilized in divinatory practices, such as tea leaf reading, pendulum work, or creating herbal blends for scrying. Additionally, many witches incorporate herbalism into their craft, using plants for their medicinal and healing properties. Herbal remedies, potions, and salves are created to address physical ailments, enhance spiritual well-being, or promote emotional balance.

Nature Connection: Working with herbs and plants in witchcraft deepens the practitioner's connection with nature and the cycles of life. It allows witches to cultivate a relationship with the plant kingdom, honoring the wisdom and energies they offer. The act of growing, harvesting, and foraging for herbs and plants also promotes a sense of reverence and gratitude for the natural world.

It is important to note that the usage of herbs and plants in witchcraft should be approached with respect, ethical considerations, and proper knowledge. Researching the properties, lore, and potential interactions of herbs is crucial to ensure safe and responsible practices. Ultimately, herbs and plants in witchcraft serve as potent allies, embodying the energies of nature and offering witches a wide range of tools for symbolic expression, magical workings, and spiritual connection.

Understanding Rituals

Casting the Circle:
Before conducting rituals or spells, witches often cast a sacred circle. This ritual creates a consecrated space where they can connect with the divine, work magic, and protect against unwanted energies. The circle acts as a boundary between the mundane and the spiritual realms.

Casting the Circle is a fundamental practice in witchcraft and ritual magic. It is a ritualistic act that creates a sacred space, separates it from the mundane world, and establishes a boundary where the practitioner can work with energy, commune with spirits, or perform spells.

Preparation: Before casting the circle, the practitioner typically gathers the necessary tools and items for the ritual. This may include candles, an altar, ritual tools (such as an athame or wand), herbs, crystals, and any specific objects or symbols associated with the intention of the ritual.

Cleansing and Purification: The practitioner may choose to cleanse and purify the space and themselves before casting the circle. This can be done through various methods, such as smudging with sacred herbs like sage or using consecrated water or salt to sprinkle or cleanse the area.

Grounding and Centering: Grounding and centering techniques help the practitioner connect with their inner self and establish a focused and balanced state of mind. This is often done through deep breathing, visualization, or meditation.

Marking the Circle: The practitioner begins by physically marking the boundaries of the circle. This can be done by walking around the designated area, either clockwise or counterclockwise, using a ritual tool to trace an imaginary or physical boundary. Some practitioners may choose to mark the circle with symbols or candles placed at the cardinal directions.

Invoking the Elements: Once the circle is physically marked, the practitioner typically invokes the elements at each cardinal direction. This may involve calling upon the energies and qualities associated with the elements of Earth (north), Air (east), Fire (south), and Water (west). Some traditions may also include a fifth element, such as Spirit or Akasha, which represents the divine or higher consciousness.

Setting Intentions and Protection: As the circle is cast, the practitioner often sets intentions for the ritual or spell work. This can be done through spoken words, affirmations, or silent visualization. Additionally, many witches invoke protective energies or entities to safeguard the sacred space and ensure that only positive energies and spirits enter the circle.

*Ritual Work***:** Once the circle is cast, the practitioner is within a consecrated space where they can perform various ritual activities. This can include spellcasting, divination, meditation, communion with spirits or deities, energy work, or any other form of magical practice aligned with their intentions.

*Closing the Circle***:** When the ritual or magical work is complete, the practitioner typically closes the circle. This is done by reversing the process of casting the circle, starting from the last cardinal direction invoked and moving counterclockwise or in the opposite direction. The practitioner may express gratitude, offer thanks to the elements or deities invoked, and release the energy that was raised within the circle.

It is important to note that the specific techniques and rituals for Casting the Circle can vary among different traditions and individual practitioners. The above description provides a general overview of the process and can be adapted to suit personal beliefs and preferences. The casting of the circle serves as a sacred and intentional act that establishes a dedicated space for magical workings and spiritual connection.

Ritual Baths

Ritual baths are a widespread practice in witchcraft. They involve cleansing the body and mind, often using specially prepared herbal infusions, salts, or essential oils. Ritual baths are performed to purify, ground, and prepare oneself for magical workings.

A witch's ritual bath is a sacred and intentional bathing practice that is often performed before rituals, spellcasting, or other spiritual practices. It is a way to cleanse and purify both the physical body and the energetic or spiritual self.

Preparation: Before beginning the ritual bath, gather the necessary items and create a sacred and serene atmosphere in your bathroom. You may want to dim the lights, light candles, and play soft, soothing music to enhance the ambiance.

Cleansing the Bath Space: Cleanse the bathtub or basin with saltwater or a herbal infusion. This clears the space of any residual energies and sets the stage for a sacred experience.

Selecting Bath Ingredients: Choose bath ingredients that align with your intention and the purpose of the ritual bath. These can include herbs, essential oils, crystals, flowers, or salts. Research the properties and correspondences of different ingredients to find ones that resonate with your desired outcome.

Charging the Bath Water: Fill the bathtub or basin with warm water. As you do so, infuse the water with your intention and visualize it being charged with positive and transformative energy. You can speak words of affirmation or use a mantra during this process.

Adding Ritual Ingredients: Add the selected ritual ingredients to the bathwater. You may sprinkle in dried herbs, a few drops of essential oils, flower petals, or a handful of bath salts. Stir the water gently with your hand to distribute the ingredients and allow their energies to merge with the water.

Cleansing Ritual: Before entering the bath, stand beside the tub and take a few moments to ground and center yourself. You may choose to light incense, smudge yourself with sage, or perform a quick energy cleansing ritual using your hands or a ritual tool. This step helps to release any negativity or stagnant energy from your auric field.

Stepping into the Bath: Slowly immerse yourself in the bathwater, feeling it enveloping your body. Allow yourself to relax and let go of any tension or stress. Take deep breaths and focus on the sensations of the water, the scents, and the energy of the ingredients.

Visualization and Intention: As you soak in the bath, visualize the water and the ingredients working their magic. Hold your intention clearly in your mind and feel the energy of the ingredients merging with your own. You may recite affirmations or chants related to your intention to amplify its power.

Reflection and Meditation: Use this time in the bath to reflect on your desires, goals, and spiritual journey. You can meditate, journal, or simply be present with your thoughts and emotions. Allow the water to cleanse your mind, body, and spirit, promoting a sense of clarity and renewal.

Closing the Ritual: When you feel ready, slowly rise from the bathwater, feeling the energy of the ritual still enveloping you. Take a moment to express gratitude for the experience and for the elements and energies that supported you. You can drain the bathwater, knowing that any residual energies are being released.

Post-Bath Self-Care: After the ritual bath, take time to care for yourself. Wrap yourself in a soft towel or robe, moisturize your skin, and continue to nurture your body and spirit. Drink plenty of water to stay hydrated and engage in activities that promote relaxation and self-care.

Remember, the specific ingredients and rituals used in a witch's ritual bath can vary based on personal preference, tradition, and the intention of the ritual. The key is to approach the bath with mindfulness, reverence, and a connection to your own inner magic.

Sabbats and Esbats

Witches celebrate seasonal festivals known as Sabbats and honor the phases of the moon during Esbats. Sabbats mark significant points in the wheel of the year, such as Samhain, Beltane, or Yule. Esbats focus on lunar energies and are observed during the full and new moon.

Witches Sabbats and Esbats are significant occasions in the practice of witchcraft and paganism. They mark the cycles of the seasons and the phases of the moon, providing opportunities for celebration, ritual, and spiritual connection. Here is an extensive description of these important witchcraft events:

Sabbats: Sabbats are the eight major seasonal festivals celebrated by witches and pagans throughout the year. They are aligned with the Wheel of the Year, which represents the cycle of nature's seasons and the corresponding energies. The Sabbats are typically divided into two categories: the Lesser Sabbats, also known as the Equinoxes and Solstices, and the Greater Sabbats, which are based on agricultural and folk traditions. Each Sabbat carries its own themes, symbolism, and rituals.

The Lesser Sabbats: The Lesser Sabbats, also known as the Wheel of the Year Sabbats, include the following:

Samhain: Celebrated on October 31st or November 1st, Samhain marks the end of the harvest season and the beginning of the dark half of the year. It is a time to honor ancestors, remember loved ones who have passed, and embrace the cycle of death and rebirth.

Imbolc: Celebrated on February 1st or 2nd, Imbolc heralds the return of spring and the awakening of the earth. It is a time to honor the goddess Brigid, cleanse and purify, and set intentions for the coming season.

Ostara: Celebrated on the Vernal Equinox, around March 20th, Ostara celebrates the arrival of spring and the balance between light and darkness. It is a time of fertility, growth, and new beginnings.

Beltane: Celebrated on May 1st, Beltane welcomes the full arrival of spring and the blossoming of nature. It is a celebration of fertility, passion, and the union of the god and goddess.

Litha: Celebrated on the Summer Solstice, around June 21st, Litha honors the height of summer and the longest day of the year. It is a time to celebrate the sun, embrace abundance, and connect with the energy of fire.

Lammas/Lughnasadh: Celebrated on August 1st, Lammas marks the first harvest of the year and the abundance of the growing season. It is a time to give thanks for the fruits of labor, share in community, and prepare for the coming autumn.

Mabon: Celebrated on the Autumnal Equinox, around September 21st, Mabon signifies the second harvest and the balance between light and darkness. It is a time to express gratitude, harvest blessings, and prepare for the introspective season.

The Greater Sabbats: The Greater Sabbats include the following:

Yule: Celebrated on the Winter Solstice, around December 21st, Yule marks the rebirth of the sun and the return of light. It is a time of introspection, renewal, and celebrating the return of longer days.

Midsummer: Celebrated on the Summer Solstice, around June 21st, Midsummer honors the power of the sun and the peak of summer. It is a time for outdoor rituals, bonfires, and connecting with the energy of nature.

Esbats: Esbats are the monthly lunar rituals observed by witches and pagans. They typically take place during the Full Moon and sometimes the New Moon. Esbats are opportunities for reflection, manifestation, and working with lunar energies. Each Full Moon and New Moon has its own unique qualities and associations, offering different focuses for magical workings and rituals.

Full Moon Esbats: Full Moon Esbats are held when the moon is at its fullest and brightest. They are associated with heightened energy, illumination, and the culmination of intentions. Full Moon rituals often involve spells for manifestation, divination, and healing.

New Moon Esbats: New Moon Esbats occur when the moon is in its darkest phase, and the night sky is devoid of visible moonlight. They are associated with new beginnings, setting intentions, and planting seeds of growth. New Moon rituals often involve introspection, meditation, and intention-setting practices.

During both Sabbats and Esbats, witches may gather in groups or perform solitary rituals. Rituals can include casting circles, invoking deities or spirits, working with elements, performing divination, spellcasting, and honoring specific themes and energies associated with the occasion. The specific rituals and practices may vary based on individual traditions, beliefs, and intentions.

Overall, Sabbats and Esbats play a crucial role in the witchcraft and pagan traditions, providing opportunities to connect with nature, honor the cycles of life, and tap into the powerful energies of the seasons and the moon. They offer a framework for spiritual practice, personal growth, and the celebration of the interconnectedness of all things.

Spell work: Witches use spells to manifest their intentions, desires, and goals. Spells can involve the use of candles, crystals, herbs, written affirmations, and other tools. They are performed with focused intent, visualization, and the raising of energy to bring about a desired outcome.

Witch's spell work is an integral part of witchcraft practice, encompassing a wide range of techniques and rituals used to manifest desires, create change, and harness personal power. Here is an extensive description of witch's spell work:

Intent and Focus: Spells begin with a clear intention. The witch focuses their energy and thoughts on their desired outcome. Clarity of intent is crucial as it directs the energy towards a specific goal.

Correspondences: Witches often work with correspondences, which are symbolic associations between objects, elements, colors, herbs, crystals, moon phases, and more. These correspondences align with specific intentions and enhance the power of spells. For example, using rose quartz for love spells or burning lavender for relaxation and healing.

Tools and Rituals: Witches may use various tools and ritual practices to enhance their spell work. Some common tools include candles, herbs, crystals, athames (ritual knives), wands, cauldrons, and written or spoken incantations. These tools are used to focus and direct energy, create sacred space, and invoke the desired energies.

Casting the Circle: Before spell work, witches often cast a sacred circle. This ritual involves creating an energetic boundary around themselves or their working area. The circle acts as a protective space, containing and amplifying the energy raised during the spell. It can be cast using physical objects, visualization, or a combination of both.

Energy Manipulation: Witches work with various forms of energy, such as personal energy, elemental energy, lunar energy, or divine energy. They may visualize, raise, and direct this energy through different techniques, including meditation, breathwork, visualization, or physical movement. The focused energy is then infused into the spell's intention.

Spell Components: Spells often involve the use of specific components aligned with the intention, such as herbs, oils, crystals, sigils, written spells, or sacred objects. These components are carefully chosen based on their correspondences and the desired outcome of the spell. They are used to enhance and amplify the spell's energy.

Ritual Timing: Witches may consider timing when casting spells. They may align their spell work with specific moon phases, planetary alignments, or astrological events. Timing can enhance the potency of the spell and synchronize it with natural cycles and cosmic energies.

Visualization and Focus: Visualization is a vital aspect of spell work. Witches often use their imagination and mental imagery to vividly envision their desired outcome. They focus their intention and energy on this visualization, believing that the power of the mind influences reality.

Incantations and Chants: Witches may use spoken or written incantations and chants to amplify their intentions and raise energy. These words, often rhyming or rhythmic, carry symbolic meaning and help to align the witch's consciousness with the desired outcome.

Release and Trust: Once the spell work is completed, witches release the energy and intention into the universe, trusting that it will manifest in the best way possible. They let go of attachment to the outcome, allowing the spell to unfold and align with the greater forces at work.

It's important to note that spell work is a deeply personal practice, and the techniques and rituals used may vary among individuals and traditions. The effectiveness of spell work relies on the witch's connection to their intuition, personal energy, and belief in their power to create change. Ethical considerations and a respectful approach to working with energies and entities are also fundamental aspects of witch's spell work.

Divination: Divination practices, such as tarot card readings, scrying, or rune casting, are used by witches to gain insight, guidance, and spiritual messages. Divination is a means of connecting with the higher self, spirit guides, or the divine to seek answers and wisdom.

Witch's divination is the practice of seeking knowledge and insight through various methods to gain understanding, guidance, and foresight. Divination allows witches to tap into their intuition, connect with spiritual realms, and access hidden information.

Tarot Reading: Tarot reading is a widely practiced form of divination that holds a significant place in witchcraft and occult traditions. It involves the use of a deck of Tarot cards, which are rich in symbolism and imagery, to gain insights, guidance, and spiritual understanding.

The Tarot deck consists of 78 cards, divided into two main sections: the Major Arcana and the Minor Arcana. The Major Arcana comprises 22 cards, representing archetypal energies and significant life events. These cards often depict powerful figures, such as The Fool, The Magician, The High Priestess, and The World. The Minor Arcana consists of 56 cards, divided into four suits (Cups, Pentacles, Swords, and Wands), each associated with different aspects of life, emotions, material matters, and intellect.

Tarot reading as a form of divination involves the following elements:

1. Intuition and Connection: The Tarot reader establishes a connection with the cards and taps into their intuition. Through focused concentration and meditation, the reader attunes to the energies of the Tarot deck and the person or situation being explored.

2. Questioning and Spreads: The person seeking the reading typically poses a specific question or seeks guidance on a particular area of their life. The Tarot reader then selects a spread, which is a specific arrangement of cards, to address the question or provide insights. Common spreads include the Celtic Cross, Three-Card Spread, or the Past-Present-Future Spread.

3. Interpretation: Each Tarot card holds its own symbolism and meaning, which is interpreted by the reader based on the question, the position of the card in the spread, and their intuitive insights. The reader considers the imagery, the card's position, its relationship to other cards, and their personal knowledge of Tarot symbolism to derive meaning and messages.

4. Symbolic Language and Archetypes: The Tarot deck is a repository of archetypal images and symbols that tap into the collective unconscious. The reader interprets the cards based on these archetypes and their symbolic representations, providing guidance, insight, and potential outcomes related to the question or situation at hand.

5. Personal Empowerment and Self-Reflection: Tarot readings encourage personal empowerment and self-reflection. The cards serve as a mirror, reflecting one's inner thoughts, emotions, patterns, and potential paths. Through the insights gained from a Tarot reading, individuals can gain clarity, make informed decisions, and navigate their life's journey with a deeper understanding of themselves and the energies at play.

Tarot reading in witchcraft is not just about fortune-telling but is also a tool for personal growth, spiritual exploration, and connecting with higher realms of consciousness. It is a means to access guidance from the spiritual realm, the collective unconscious, and one's higher self.

It is important to note that Tarot reading requires practice, knowledge of the cards, and a respectful approach to the Tarot's symbolism and spiritual significance. It is a skill that develops over time, with continued study, intuition, and experience.

Overall, Tarot reading has become a popular form of divination in witchcraft due to its versatility, rich symbolism, and capacity to offer profound insights and guidance. It serves as a valuable tool for self-discovery, personal empowerment, and spiritual exploration within the context of witchcraft practices.

Oracle Reading: Oracle reading is another popular form of divination in witchcraft that involves seeking guidance and insights through the use of oracle decks. Oracle cards are similar to Tarot cards but often have their own unique themes, imagery, and interpretations. Oracle decks can range from simple affirmation cards to more complex systems with specific messages or symbolism.

1. Intuitive Guidance: Oracle reading relies heavily on intuition and personal connection to the cards. The reader enters a meditative state and connects with their higher self or spirit guides to receive messages and guidance through the oracle deck. This intuitive approach allows for a personalized and individualized reading.

2. Diverse Deck Themes: Oracle decks come in various themes, such as angels, animals, nature, goddesses, or elemental energies. Each deck has its own unique symbolism and messages associated with the theme. The reader selects a deck based on their intuitive pull or the specific energy they want to connect with during the reading.

3. Card Interpretation: Oracle cards typically feature a single message or keyword on each card. The reader interprets the meaning of the cards based on their intuition, the symbolism on the cards, and the specific messages associated with each card in the deck. Some oracle decks may come with a guidebook that provides additional insights and interpretations.

4. Personal Reflection and Empowerment: Oracle readings often encourage personal reflection and self-empowerment. The cards serve as

prompts or invitations to delve deeper into one's thoughts, emotions, and experiences. They can provide clarity, guidance, and inspiration, helping individuals gain a deeper understanding of themselves and their current situations.

5. Affirmation and Healing: Many oracle decks focus on providing affirmations, positive messages, and healing energies. They can be used as a tool for self-care, emotional support, and personal growth. Oracle readings can offer comfort, encouragement, and reassurance during challenging times.

6. Flexible and Intuitive Spreads: While some oracle decks may have suggested spreads, oracle readings often offer more flexibility in terms of spread options. Readers may choose to draw a single card for daily guidance or use custom spreads based on the specific question or intention. The intuitive approach allows for adaptability and creativity in creating spreads.

7. Combination with Other Divination Methods: Oracle readings can be used in conjunction with other divination methods, such as Tarot cards, pendulum work, or scrying. They can complement and enhance other forms of divination, providing additional insights and perspectives.

Oracle reading in witchcraft divination offers a flexible, intuitive, and personalized approach to seeking guidance and insights. It taps into the individual's intuition, connects them with higher realms, and provides messages, affirmations, and healing energies to support their spiritual journey. It is a tool for self-reflection, empowerment, and connection with divine energies within the context of witchcraft practices.

Runes: Runes are ancient symbols used in divination, magic, and witchcraft. They are part of the runic alphabet, known as the Elder Futhark, which consists of twenty-four symbols, each with its own name and associated meaning. Runic divination involves casting or drawing runes to gain insights, guidance, and spiritual understanding.

1. Symbolism and Meaning: Each rune has its own symbolic meaning, often connected to natural elements, deities, or concepts. For example, the rune Fehu represents wealth and abundance, while Ansuz symbolizes communication and divine inspiration. The symbolism and meanings of runes are derived from Norse mythology, cultural beliefs, and ancient wisdom.

2. Casting and Drawing: Runic divination can be performed by casting or drawing runes. Casting involves randomly scattering the runes onto a cloth or a designated surface and interpreting the ones that catch your attention or fall in specific patterns. Drawing involves selecting runes from a bag or a set and interpreting their meanings one by one. The method used can vary based on personal preference and tradition.

3. Interpretation: When interpreting runes, the practitioner considers the individual meanings of each rune as well as their relationships with one another. The position of the rune, its orientation, and the surrounding runes may also influence the interpretation. The practitioner relies on intuition, symbolism, personal insight, and knowledge of runic lore to derive meaning and messages from the runes.

4. Personal Connection and Energy: Before performing a runic divination, it is common to establish a connection with the runes. This can be done through meditation, visualization, or creating a sacred space. The practitioner may also infuse the runes with their own energy or seek the assistance of a deity or spirit guide to enhance the accuracy and depth of the readings.

5. Divinatory Spreads: Runes can be drawn or cast individually for quick

answers to specific questions or used in more complex spreads. Spreads can range from simple *three-rune* spreads representing the past, present, and future, to more elaborate layouts that explore various aspects of a situation or provide a more comprehensive reading. The practitioner may create their own spreads or use traditional ones.

6. Practical Applications: Runic divination can provide guidance on various aspects of life, including relationships, career, personal growth, and spiritual development. It can help identify obstacles, opportunities, and potential outcomes. Runes can also be used for advice, affirmation, and exploring subconscious or hidden influences.

7. Talismanic and Magical Use: In addition to divination, runes are often used for magical purposes. Each rune carries its own energy and can be incorporated into spells, charms, or rituals to enhance their effects. Runes can be inscribed on objects, carried as talismans, or used in sigil work to manifest intentions or invoke specific qualities.

Runic divination in witchcraft is a deeply symbolic and intuitive practice that connects practitioners with ancient wisdom and spiritual forces. It offers a means of receiving guidance, exploring possibilities, and deepening one's understanding of the self and the world. Working with runes requires respect, study, and personal connection to fully harness their power and wisdom.

Scrying: Scrying is a form of divination used in witchcraft that involves gazing into a reflective or translucent surface to receive visions, messages, or insights. It is a practice that has been utilized across different cultures and traditions for centuries. Scrying is a powerful tool for connecting with the subconscious mind, the spiritual realm, and the intuitive faculties.

1. Techniques and Tools: Scrying can be performed using various techniques and tools, including:

- Water Scrying: Gazing into a bowl of water or a still body of water to perceive images or symbols.

- Crystal Ball Scrying: Gazing into a crystal ball to access intuitive insights and visions.

- Mirror Scrying: Gazing into a mirror with a dark or reflective surface to receive impressions or visions.

- Flame Scrying: Observing the flames of a candle or a fire to perceive messages or symbols.

- Smoke Scrying: Observing the shapes and movements of smoke to gain insights or symbolic meanings.

2. Preparation and Ritual: Before engaging in scrying, witches often create a sacred and conducive environment. This may involve cleansing the space, setting intentions, and invoking protective energies. Some practitioners may also use incense, candles, or specific rituals to enhance the atmosphere and focus their intent.

3. Relaxation and Trance State: Scrying requires a relaxed and receptive state of mind. Witches often engage in breathing exercises, meditation, or visualization techniques to quiet the mind, enter a trance state, and open themselves to the messages and visions that may arise during the scrying session.

4. Intuition and Symbolism: Scrying relies heavily on intuition and symbolism. As the practitioner gazes into the chosen medium, they allow their intuition to guide them. Images, symbols, or impressions may arise, and the scryer interprets them based on personal associations, symbolism, and their own psychic abilities. The interpretations may also be influenced by the scryer's knowledge of esoteric symbolism and divinatory systems.

5. Psychic Development and Spirit Communication: Scrying is considered a practice that develops psychic abilities and facilitates communication with the spiritual realm. It allows the scryer to access deeper layers of consciousness, receive messages from guides or spirits, and gain insights into past, present, or future events. It can also aid in uncovering subconscious desires, fears, or unresolved issues.

6. Personal Exploration and Divination: Scrying can be used for personal exploration and divination. The scryer may seek answers to specific questions, explore their inner psyche, or gain clarity on certain aspects of their life. Scrying can offer guidance, reveal hidden information, or provide alternative perspectives on a situation.

7. Ethical Considerations and Interpretation: As with any form of divination, ethical considerations should be taken into account when scrying. It is essential to approach scrying with respect and responsibility, honoring the boundaries of the self and the spiritual realm. The interpretations of the visions or messages received during scrying should be done carefully, considering the broader context, and taking into account the scryer's own discernment and wisdom.

Scrying in witchcraft divination offers a unique and intuitive approach to gaining insights and connecting with the spiritual realm. It is a practice that requires patience, practice, and an open mind. Through scrying, witches can access hidden knowledge, deepen their intuitive abilities, and explore the realms of consciousness beyond the physical.

Pendulum Dowsing: Pendulum dowsing is a divination technique used in witchcraft that involves working with a weighted object, typically a crystal or metal pendant attached to a chain or string. The pendulum acts as a tool to access intuitive information and receive guidance from higher realms. It is a versatile and widely practiced form of divination.

1. Pendulum Selection: The first step in pendulum dowsing is selecting a pendulum that resonates with you. Pendulums come in various materials, shapes, and sizes, such as crystals (e.g., amethyst, quartz), metals (e.g., brass, silver), or wood. Choose a pendulum that feels comfortable and aligned with your energy. Some witches have multiple pendulums for different purposes or energy work.

2. Cleansing and Charging: Before using a new pendulum or after each session, it is important to cleanse and charge it. This can be done by passing it through incense smoke, visualizing it being bathed in white light, or placing it under the moonlight or sunlight. Cleansing and charging remove any energetic residues and enhance the pendulum's effectiveness.

3. Establishing Communication: Pendulum dowsing involves establishing a communication system with the pendulum. This is typically done by asking simple yes or no questions and observing the pendulum's movements. For example, you might ask, "Show me a 'yes' response" and observe the direction the pendulum swings (e.g., clockwise, back and forth). Similarly, you can ask for a "no" response to determine the opposite movement.

4. Intentions and Focus: Before each dowsing session, set clear intentions and focus your mind on the purpose of the divination. Clearly formulate the question or topic you wish to explore. This helps to align your energy and the energy of the pendulum with the desired information and guidance.

5. Dowsing Techniques: There are various techniques for pendulum dowsing, including:

    ◦ Yes/No Questions: Use the pendulum to ask simple yes or no questions. Observe the movement and direction to receive the answer.

- Chart or Mat Dowsing: Use a dowsing chart or mat that contains different options or categories. Hold the pendulum over the chart and ask specific questions, observing where the pendulum swings or points to on the chart.

- Map Dowsing: Like chart dowsing, but instead of using a chart, you can use a map to locate specific places, energies, or information.

6. Interpreting Pendulum Movements: Interpretation of pendulum movements is subjective and may vary among individuals. Pay attention to the pendulum's swings, rotations, or vibrations. These can convey different meanings, such as affirmation, hesitation, uncertainty, or strong energy. Trust your intuition and rely on your personal experience and connection with the pendulum to decipher the messages.

7. Ethical Considerations: Like any form of divination, it is important to approach pendulum dowsing with ethical considerations. Respect boundaries, seek consent from the higher realms, and use your divination abilities responsibly. Remember that divination tools are tools for guidance, and ultimately, you have free will and personal agency in making decisions and choices.

Pendulum dowsing in witchcraft divination offers a direct and tangible way to connect with intuitive guidance and receive insights. It provides a means to access higher wisdom, explore energetic patterns, and gain clarity in various aspects of life. With practice and a focused mind, pendulum dowsing can become a valuable tool in a witch's divinatory practices and spiritual journey.

Numerology: Numerology is a divination practice that assigns symbolic meanings to numbers and utilizes calculations based on those meanings to gain insights and understanding. In the context of witchcraft, numerology is often used as a tool for divination and spiritual exploration.

1. Symbolic Meanings: Numerology assigns symbolic meanings to numbers based on their energetic vibrations and influences. Each number is believed to carry its own unique qualities, characteristics, and associations. For example, the number 1 is often associated with new beginnings and individuality, while the number 7 is connected to spirituality and introspection. These symbolic meanings form the foundation of numerology divination.

2. Calculation Methods: Numerology involves various calculation methods to gain insights and interpret the meanings of numbers. The most common calculations include reducing numbers to single digits or utilizing specific combinations of numbers. For instance, a person's birth date or name may be reduced to a single digit or analyzed for specific patterns or combinations that hold significance.

3. Life Path Number: The life path number is one of the fundamental aspects of numerology. It is derived from a person's birth date and provides insights into their life purpose, potential challenges, and overall personality traits. By calculating and interpreting the life path number, witches can gain a deeper understanding of themselves or others.

4. Personal and Universal Year Numbers: Numerology also assigns personal year numbers and universal year numbers. Personal year numbers reflect the energy and influences that surround an individual in a specific year, providing insights into personal growth, opportunities, and challenges. Universal year numbers offer a broader perspective by representing the collective energy and trends that affect society as a whole.

5. Compatibility and Relationships: Numerology can be used to assess compatibility and understand the dynamics of relationships. By analyzing the life path numbers or other significant numbers of individuals

involved, witches can gain insights into the strengths, challenges, and compatibility of the relationship. Numerology can help identify areas of harmony or potential areas of conflict within partnerships, friendships, or familial relationships.

6. Divinatory Spreads and Interpretation: Numerology can be incorporated into divinatory spreads or readings similar to other divination systems like Tarot. Witches may create their own spreads or utilize established ones to explore different aspects of life, such as career, relationships, or personal growth. The interpretation of numerological readings relies on the intuitive abilities of the practitioner and their understanding of the symbolic meanings associated with the numbers.

7. Personal Growth and Spiritual Development: Numerology in witchcraft divination offers more than just predictions or insights into external circumstances. It can be a tool for personal growth, self-reflection, and spiritual development. By understanding the energies and lessons associated with different numbers, witches can align themselves with their inherent strengths and work on areas that require growth or healing.

Numerology as a divination practice in witchcraft provides a framework for understanding the energetic influences of numbers and their significance in various aspects of life. It offers a means to gain insights, explore personal dynamics, and navigate spiritual paths. By incorporating numerology into their divinatory practices, witches can deepen their connection with the energetic vibrations of numbers and use them as a tool for self-discovery, guidance, and spiritual exploration.

Astrology: Astrology is an ancient divination practice that examines the correlation between celestial movements and events on Earth. In the context of witchcraft, astrology is commonly used as a tool for divination, understanding personality traits, predicting future events, and gaining insights into spiritual and energetic influences.

1. Celestial Bodies and Zodiac Signs: Astrology assigns symbolic meanings to celestial bodies, including the sun, moon, planets, and asteroids. These bodies are believed to influence different aspects of life and carry specific energies and qualities. In addition, astrology divides the sky into twelve zodiac signs, each associated with particular traits and characteristics.

2. Birth Chart: The birth chart, also known as the natal chart or horoscope, is a fundamental tool in astrology. It is a map of the sky at the moment of an individual's birth and provides a snapshot of the planets' positions in relation to the zodiac signs. The birth chart serves as a personal blueprint that offers insights into a person's personality, strengths, challenges, and life path.

3. Planetary Aspects: Astrology considers the relationships and angles formed between the planets in a birth chart, known as aspects. These aspects, such as conjunctions, oppositions, and trines, indicate how different energies interact and influence each other. They provide information about potential strengths, challenges, and opportunities in a person's life.

4. Houses: Astrology divides the birth chart into twelve houses, each representing a different area of life, such as career, relationships, home, or spirituality. The placement of planets within these houses provides insights into the specific areas of focus and potential experiences in an individual's life journey.

5. Transits: Astrological transits refer to the current positions of the planets and their aspects to an individual's birth chart. By analyzing transits, witches can gain insights into the energies and influences at play in the

present and future. Transits can be used to predict events, understand potential challenges or opportunities, and make informed decisions.

6. Lunar Phases: The moon's phases play a significant role in astrology and witchcraft. Each lunar phase is associated with different energies and intentions. Witches often align their rituals, spell work, and divination practices with the lunar cycle, utilizing the waxing, full, and waning moon energies for specific purposes.

7. Predictive Astrology: Astrology can be used for predictive purposes, offering insights into future events, trends, and energetic influences. Predictive techniques, such as progressions and solar returns, allow witches to track the ongoing evolution of an individual's life and make predictions based on the movement of celestial bodies.

8. Astrological Compatibility: Astrology also provides a framework for assessing compatibility between individuals. By comparing birth charts, witches can analyze the compatibility of personalities, relationships, and potential challenges within partnerships, friendships, or family dynamics.

9. Archetypal Symbolism: Astrology incorporates archetypal symbolism, drawing from mythology, ancient wisdom, and cultural references. These symbols add depth and nuance to astrological interpretations, allowing witches to tap into collective knowledge and shared experiences.

10. Spiritual and Self-Exploration: Astrology in witchcraft divination goes beyond predictions and external events. It serves as a tool for self-exploration, spiritual growth, and understanding the interconnectedness of cosmic energies. Astrology offers a language to explore one's strengths, challenges, and soul's journey, aiding in personal and spiritual development.

Astrology in witchcraft divination provides a holistic framework for understanding the energetic influences of celestial bodies and their impact on individual lives. It offers a means to gain insights, predict trends, and explore the intricate connections between the microcosm (individual) and macrocosm (universe). By incorporating astrology into their divinatory practices, witches can deepen their understanding of cosmic energies, tap into ancient wisdom, and navigate their spiritual paths with greater awareness and guidance.

Tea Leaf Reading: Teal leaf reading, also known as tasseography or tea leaf reading, is a form of divination that involves interpreting patterns formed by tea leaves or tea residue left in a cup after drinking. It is an ancient practice that has been used for centuries in different cultures, including within the realm of witchcraft. Here is an extensive description of teal leaf reading in witchcraft:

1. Preparation: To practice teal leaf reading, you will need a cup or teapot, loose tea leaves, boiling water, and a saucer. It's important to choose a tea that resonates with your intention or the type of information you wish to seek. Herbal teas or blends with symbolic properties may be particularly suitable for magical or ritualistic purposes.

2. Brewing the Tea: Begin by brewing a cup of tea using loose tea leaves. Infuse the leaves in the boiling water for the recommended time. As you prepare the tea, focus your intentions, and visualize the energy of the tea leaves infusing with your desired outcome or the question you want to explore.

3. Drinking the Tea: While enjoying your cup of tea, it's essential to be mindful of your thoughts, feelings, and the sensory experience. Allow yourself to relax and be open to any impressions or insights that may arise. Some practitioners prefer to stir the tea leaves in a clockwise or counterclockwise direction with a spoon before drinking to further infuse their energy into the cup.

4. Leaf Reading Process: Once you have finished drinking the tea, leave a small amount of liquid in the cup. Swirl the cup gently in a circular motion to distribute the tea leaves along the sides and bottom. Then, carefully turn the cup upside down onto the saucer, allowing the excess liquid to drain out. This leaves the tea leaves stuck to the sides and bottom of the cup, forming various shapes and patterns.

5. Interpretation: The next step is to interpret the shapes, symbols, and patterns formed by the tea leaves. Use your intuition and observation skills to discern any meaningful images or symbols. These can include objects, animals, numbers, letters, or abstract shapes. Pay attention to both individual symbols and their placement in relation to each other.

6. Symbolic Meanings: The interpretation of the tea leaf symbols will largely depend on your personal intuitive understanding and the symbolic meanings associated with different shapes and objects. Some common interpretations include leaves representing growth or change, birds indicating messages or freedom, and circles symbolizing completion or unity. It can be helpful to keep a journal or reference guide to record and explore different symbol interpretations.

7. Contextual Interpretation: To further enhance the accuracy of your readings, consider the context in which the tea leaf symbols appear. Take into account the question or intention you had in mind, your current circumstances, and any specific concerns or energies you are working with. This context can provide additional insights and nuances to the overall reading.

8. Ritual and Magic: Tea leaf reading in witchcraft can also be incorporated into rituals or magical practices. You can infuse your tea preparation with specific intentions, call upon deities or spirits for guidance, or create sacred space before conducting the reading. It can be helpful to develop your own rituals and practices that align with your personal beliefs and

magical traditions.

Teal leaf reading in witchcraft divination offers a unique and intuitive way to gain insights, explore symbols, and connect with the energies of the natural world. It allows witches to tap into their own psychic abilities and the wisdom of the tea leaves to receive guidance, messages, or confirmations on their spiritual path. With practice and a receptive mindset, teal leaf reading can become a valuable tool for divination and self-exploration within the realm of witchcraft.

Candle Reading: Candle reading, also known as ceromancy, is a form of divination in which the shape, behavior, and residue of a burning candle are interpreted to gain insights, guidance, and messages. It is a widely practiced and versatile form of divination within witchcraft. Here is an extensive description of candle reading in witchcraft divination:

1. Selecting the Candle: Choose a candle that resonates with your intention or the specific aspect of your life you wish to explore. Different candle colors are associated with different energies and intentions. For example, white represents purity and spiritual connection, red symbolizes passion and vitality, and green signifies abundance and healing. Select a candle that aligns with your purpose.

2. Preparing the Candle: Before beginning the candle reading, it is essential to cleanse and consecrate the candle. This can be done through various methods such as smudging, passing the candle through incense smoke, or anointing it with oils or herbs that correspond to your intention. These steps help to energetically align the candle with your purpose and clear any unwanted energies.

3. Setting Intentions: Prior to lighting the candle, set clear intentions for the reading. Focus your mind and visualize the specific question or area of life you want guidance on. Formulate your intention as a concise

statement or affirmation, and hold it in your mind as you proceed with the reading.

4. Lighting the Candle: Carefully light the candle while keeping your intention in mind. As the flame flickers and grows, it is believed to connect with the spiritual realm and serve as a channel for receiving messages and insights. Take a moment to observe the flame, its color, and its behavior. Note any initial impressions or intuitive feelings that arise.

5. Flame Interpretation: The behavior of the candle flame is a key element in candle reading. Pay attention to factors such as the height, intensity, direction, and movement of the flame. A steady and vibrant flame generally indicates a positive and focused energy, while a weak or erratic flame may suggest challenges or obstacles. Use your intuition to interpret the flame's message in relation to your intention and question.

6. Candle Wax and Residue: As the candle burns, it may produce various patterns, shapes, and formations with its wax and residue. These formations are often considered significant in candle reading. Observe the wax pool, any drippings, and the shapes that appear. Look for recognizable symbols, figures, or patterns that may provide insights or messages. It can be helpful to take photographs or make sketches to document these formations for later interpretation.

7. Extinguishing the Candle: Once you have completed the reading or when you feel it is appropriate, extinguish the candle. Use a candle snuffer or carefully blow it out, focusing on your gratitude for the guidance and messages received. It is important to close the reading consciously and respectfully, thanking any spiritual entities or energies that may have been present during the divination.

8. Interpretation and Reflection: After the candle reading, spend time reflecting on the observations, symbols, and messages that emerged. Com-

pare them to your initial intention and question. Interpret the candle's behavior and wax formations in the context of your own intuitive understanding and the symbolic meanings associated with candles and fire. Journaling about your experiences can help deepen your understanding and track any recurring patterns or themes that arise in future readings.

9. Integration and Action: Candle reading is not just about receiving messages; it is also a call to action. Reflect on the guidance received and consider how you can apply it in your life. Take any necessary steps or make appropriate changes based on the insights gained from the reading. Remember that divination is a tool for self-reflection and empowerment, and it is up to you to act upon the guidance received.

Candle reading in witchcraft divination offers a tangible and visual way to connect with spiritual energies and receive guidance. It combines the symbolism of candles, the element of fire, and intuitive interpretation to gain insights into various aspects of life. With practice and a receptive mindset, candle reading can become a powerful tool for self-discovery, manifestation, and spiritual growth within the realm of witchcraft.

Spirit Communication: Witches may practice spirit communication to receive guidance and messages from spirits, ancestors, or spirit guides. This can be done through meditation, mediumship, or channeling. Witches establish a connection with the spiritual realm to receive insights, advice, or warnings.

Dream Interpretation: Dream interpretation is a customary practice in witchcraft divination that involves analyzing the symbols, emotions, and narratives that arise in dreams to gain insights into the subconscious mind, receive messages from the spiritual realm, and uncover hidden truths. Dreams are seen as a doorway to the unconscious, where deep-seated thoughts, desires, fears, and spiritual connections can be accessed.

1. Dream Recall: Developing the ability to remember and recall your dreams is an important first step in dream interpretation. Keep a dream journal by your bedside and make it a habit to record your dreams as soon as you wake up. Even fleeting images or emotions can hold valuable information for interpretation.

2. Symbolic Analysis: In dream interpretation, symbols play a significant role. Symbols can be objects, people, animals, locations, or abstract concepts that appear in your dreams. Pay attention to the specific symbols that stand out and explore their potential meanings. Remember that the meaning of symbols can vary based on personal associations and cultural or archetypal significance.

3. Emotional and Sensory Awareness: Alongside symbols, emotions and sensations experienced in dreams provide important clues for interpretation. Consider the emotions you felt during the dream and how they relate to the overall narrative or symbolism. Reflect on any sensory experiences, such as taste, touch, smell, and sound, as they can offer additional insights into the dream's meaning.

4. Personal Associations: Dream interpretation is highly individualistic. Consider your personal associations with the symbols, images, and themes in your dreams. Reflect on how they relate to your waking life, experiences, and subconscious thoughts. Look for patterns or recurring symbols that may hold special significance for you.

5. Archetypal and Universal Symbols: Dreams often tap into collective or archetypal symbolism. Explore the archetypal meanings associated with certain symbols and how they connect to universal human experiences and collective consciousness. Familiarize yourself with common symbols and their potential interpretations across many cultures and spiritual traditions.

6. Intuition and Intuitive Insights: Trust your intuition when interpreting dreams. While reference materials and symbolism guides can be helpful, your own intuitive insights and personal connection to the dream are equally important. Pay attention to your immediate reactions, gut feelings, and intuitive hunches about the dream's message and significance.

7. Context and Personal Growth: Dream interpretation is not limited to individual symbols alone. Consider the larger context of the dream, including the narrative, interactions, and themes. Reflect on how the dream relates to your current life circumstances, challenges, or goals. Dreams often offer guidance, warnings, or suggestions for personal growth and transformation.

8. Ritual and Dream Incubation: Witches may incorporate dream interpretation into their rituals and magical practices. They may create dream altars, use specific herbs or crystals for dream enhancement, or perform dream incubation rituals to encourage specific dreams or seek guidance from specific deities or spirits. These rituals can help deepen the connection to the dream realm and enhance the clarity and potency of the dream messages.

9. Integration and Application: After interpreting your dreams, take time to reflect on the insights and messages received. Consider how you can apply this wisdom to your waking life, spiritual practice, or personal development. Dreams can provide guidance, validation, and inspiration for decision-making, problem-solving, and spiritual exploration.

10. Dream Journaling and Tracking: Keep a consistent dream journal to track your dreams over time. Look for patterns, recurring symbols, or themes that emerge across multiple dreams. Journaling helps establish a deeper understanding of your personal dream symbolism and allows you to track your spiritual and personal growth journey through dreams.

Dream interpretation in witchcraft divination is a dynamic and intuitive process that invites witches to explore the rich symbolism of their dreams, access their subconscious mind, and connect with the spiritual realm. By cultivating dream awareness and developing the skills of interpretation, witches can unlock profound insights, receive guidance, and deepen their understanding of themselves and the world around them.

Cartomancy: Cartomancy is a form of divination that uses a deck of cards for intuitive insights, guidance, and prediction. While it is not exclusive to witchcraft, cartomancy is a popular and versatile practice within the realm of witchcraft divination. Here is an extensive description of cartomancy in witchcraft:

1. Card Deck: Cartomancy can be practiced with various types of card decks, including traditional playing cards, oracle cards, or tarot cards. The choice of deck depends on personal preference and the specific system of symbolism you resonate with. Each deck has its own set of meanings and symbolism associated with the cards.

2. Cleansing and Consecration: Before using the card deck for divination, it is recommended to cleanse and consecrate the cards. This process removes any energetic imprints and establishes a sacred connection. Cleansing can be done through smudging, passing the cards through incense smoke, or using other purification rituals. Consecration involves setting intentions, infusing the cards with your energy, and inviting spiritual guidance.

3. Shuffling and Preparation: Begin by shuffling the card deck while focusing on your intention or the question you seek guidance on. You can shuffle in any way that feels natural to you, whether it's a traditional riffle shuffle, overhand shuffle, or any other method. As you shuffle, concentrate on your question and connect with the energy of the cards.

4. Card Spreads: Card spreads are specific arrangements of cards used for divination. There are numerous spreads to choose from, ranging from simple three-card spreads to more complex spreads like the Celtic Cross. Each spread serves a different purpose and offers insight into various aspects of the question or situation. Select a spread that aligns with your intention and the depth of information you seek.

5. Card Interpretation: Once you have selected and laid out the cards in the chosen spread, begin interpreting their meanings. Pay attention to the symbolism, imagery, colors, and numbers on each card. Use your intuition, knowledge of the card meanings, and personal associations to interpret the messages they convey. Consider how the cards interact with each other within the spread.

6. Intuitive Insight: In addition to the traditional meanings of the cards, trust your intuition to guide your interpretation. Allow your intuition to fill in the gaps and provide additional insights beyond the literal meanings of the cards. Intuitive insight helps you connect with your higher self, spirit guides, and the collective consciousness to receive deeper messages and guidance.

7. Contextual Analysis: Interpret the cards within the context of your specific question or situation. Consider how the cards relate to your personal circumstances, emotions, and relationships. Take note of any recurring themes or patterns that emerge across multiple cards or spreads. Contextual analysis helps you tailor the guidance to your unique circumstances.

8. Ritual and Sacred Space: Many witches incorporate ritual and sacred space into their cartomancy practice. Create a sacred space by casting a circle, calling upon deities or spirits for guidance, or performing grounding and centering exercises before conducting the reading. Ritualistic practices help establish a focused and sacred atmosphere con-

ducive to receiving spiritual messages.

9. Reflection and Integration: After the card reading, spend time reflecting on the messages and insights received. Consider how they align with your intuition and resonate with your personal journey. Contemplate the guidance provided by the cards and explore how you can integrate it into your life for personal growth, decision-making, or problem-solving.

10. Practice and Experience: Cartomancy, like any form of divination, improves with practice and experience. Regularly practice reading the cards to develop your interpretation skills, deepen your connection with the cards, and strengthen your intuitive abilities. Over time, you will become more attuned to the cards and their messages, allowing you to gain greater clarity and accuracy in your readings.

Cartomancy in witchcraft divination offers a dynamic and accessible tool for receiving guidance, exploring the energies at play, and tapping into intuitive wisdom. Through the art of card reading, witches can connect with their higher selves, spirit guides, and the collective consciousness to gain valuable insights and navigate their spiritual paths.

Crystal Divination: Crystal divination, also known as crystal scrying or crystal gazing, is a form of divination in witchcraft that utilizes crystals or gemstones as tools for receiving insights, guidance, and messages from the spiritual realm. Crystals have long been associated with mystical and metaphysical properties, and their unique energies and vibrations make them powerful conduits for divinatory practices.

1. Choosing Crystals: Select crystals that resonate with your intention or the specific aspect of your life you wish to explore. Different crystals have different energetic properties and correspondences. Some commonly used crystals for divination include clear quartz, amethyst, rose quartz,

obsidian, and labradorite. Consider the meanings and properties associated with each crystal and choose one or multiple that align with your purpose.

2. Cleansing and Charging: Before using the crystals for divination, it is essential to cleanse and charge them to remove any residual energies and establish a fresh connection. There are various methods for cleansing crystals, such as placing them under running water, smudging them with sage or palo santo, burying them in the earth, or using sound vibrations. Charging the crystals can be done by exposing them to sunlight, moonlight, or by infusing them with your intention through visualization or ritual.

3. Creating a Sacred Space: Prepare a sacred space for your crystal divination practice. Clear the area of any distractions or negative energies. You can cast a circle, create an altar, or simply set aside a dedicated space where you can focus and connect with your crystals and the spiritual realm.

4. Centering and Grounding: Before beginning the divination session, take a moment to center and ground yourself. Grounding techniques such as deep breathing, visualization, or connecting with the earth's energy help you to anchor your energy and establish a strong connection with the crystals.

5. Crystal Scrying: Place the chosen crystal in front of you or hold it in your hand. Relax your gaze and allow your eyes to softly focus on the crystal. Fixate your attention on the crystal's surface, allowing yourself to enter a meditative state. Let your mind become receptive to images, symbols, colors, or patterns that may appear on or within the crystal. Be open to receiving intuitive insights and messages.

6. Intuitive Interpretation: As you scry into the crystal, trust your intuition

to guide your interpretation of the images or symbols that arise. Pay attention to the emotions, sensations, or thoughts that accompany these visions. Reflect on their potential meanings and how they relate to your intention or the question you seek guidance on. Keep a journal to record your experiences, interpretations, and any recurring themes or symbols.

7. Crystal Grids and Layouts: In addition to scrying, crystals can be used in various layouts or grid formations for divination. Crystal grids involve placing multiple crystals in specific patterns or formations to enhance and focus their energies for divinatory purposes. Explore different crystal grid layouts that resonate with your intention and adapt them to your personal practice.

8. Communication with Spirit Guides: Crystals can serve as portals for communication with spirit guides, ancestors, or higher beings. During your crystal divination practice, you can invite the presence of these entities and ask for their guidance and wisdom. Establish a connection through meditation, prayer, or specific rituals that resonate with your beliefs and practices.

9. Reflection and Integration: After completing the crystal divination session, take time to reflect on the insights, images, and messages received. Consider how they align with your intuition and resonate with your personal journey. Contemplate the guidance provided by the crystals and explore how you can integrate it into your life for personal growth, decision-making, or spiritual development.

10. Care and Maintenance: Crystals are sacred tools and should be treated with care and respect. Cleanse and recharge your crystals regularly to maintain their energetic integrity. Store them in a safe and dedicated space, such as a pouch or a special box, to keep them protected and energetically aligned.

Crystal divination in witchcraft offers a profound way to connect with the wisdom of the Earth, the energies of the crystals, and the guidance of the spiritual realm. Through this practice, witches can gain valuable insights, explore their intuition, and deepen their spiritual connections.

Palmistry: Palmistry, also known as chiromancy, is a form of divination that involves analyzing the lines, shapes, and other features of the palm to gain insights into a person's personality traits, potential, and future. While it is not exclusive to witchcraft, palmistry is a popular and versatile practice within the realm of divination. Here is an extensive description of palmistry in witchcraft divination:

1. Palm Reading Basics: Palmistry involves examining the lines, mounts, shapes, and other features of the palm, as well as the fingers and nails. Each of these aspects carries specific meanings and can offer insights into different aspects of a person's life, such as their personality, relationships, career, and health.

2. Reading the Lines: The palm is characterized by various lines, including the life line, head line, heart line, fate line, and many others. Each line has its own significance and provides information about different aspects of a person's life. For example, the life line represents vitality and longevity, the head line indicates intellect and mental abilities, and the heart line reflects emotional well-being and relationships.

3. Interpreting the Mounts: Mounts are the fleshy areas on the palm, each associated with a particular planet and representing specific qualities and attributes. For instance, the mount of Venus is associated with love, creativity, and sensuality, while the mount of Jupiter represents ambition, leadership, and spirituality. The interpretation of the mounts provides further insights into a person's character and potential.

4. Finger Analysis: The fingers also hold significant meaning in palmistry.

Each finger is associated with a different element and represents various aspects of life. The length, shape, and flexibility of the fingers can offer insights into a person's personality traits, communication style, and even their approach to relationships and decision-making.

5. Nail Examination: The shape, color, and condition of the nails can provide additional clues in palmistry. For example, brittle nails may indicate physical weakness or health issues, while well-groomed and healthy nails can signify good overall well-being. The examination of nails can complement the overall reading and offer additional insights.

6. Intuition and Empathy: As with any divinatory practice, palmistry in witchcraft relies on intuition and empathy. A skilled palm reader not only observes the physical features of the palm but also tunes into the energy and vibrations emanating from the person's hand. Intuition helps to interpret the information gathered from the lines, shapes, and features, providing a more holistic understanding of the individual's situation.

7. Ritual and Sacred Space: Many witches incorporate ritual and create a sacred space when practicing palmistry. This can involve cleansing and consecrating the hands, using specific oils or herbs to enhance the psychic connection, and calling upon deities or spirit guides for guidance and protection. Ritualistic practices help establish a focused and sacred atmosphere conducive to receiving spiritual messages.

8. Ethical Considerations: In palmistry, it is important to approach the practice with respect and integrity. Practitioners should always obtain the person's consent before conducting a reading and should provide a safe and non-judgmental space for the individual to share their concerns and questions. It is essential to remember that palmistry offers insights and possibilities, but it does not determine or predict a person's destiny with absolute certainty.

9. Integration and Application: After the palm reading, it is crucial to reflect on the insights and messages received. Encourage the person to explore how the information resonates with their own experiences and how they can use the guidance to make informed decisions or navigate their life path. Palmistry is a tool for self-awareness and empowerment, allowing individuals to gain a deeper understanding of themselves and their potentials.

10. Continuous Learning and Practice: Palmistry is a skill that improves with practice, study, and experience. Continued learning about the lines, mounts, and features of the palm enhances the accuracy and depth of readings. Practicing on willing participants and keeping a journal of readings and interpretations helps to refine the practitioner's abilities and develop a personal connection with the art of palmistry.

Palmistry in witchcraft divination offers a unique and personal approach to understanding oneself and the energies at play in one's life. It allows witches to tap into the wisdom of the body and the spirit, offering guidance, self-discovery, and empowerment.

Bibliomancy: Bibliomancy is a form of divination that utilizes books or sacred texts as a means of seeking guidance and insight. It has a long history and is practiced in various spiritual traditions, including witchcraft. Here is an extensive description of bibliomancy in witchcraft divination:

1. Book Selection: To practice bibliomancy, you first need to choose a book or a collection of texts that you consider sacred, spiritually significant, or personally meaningful. This can be a religious scripture, a book of poetry, a philosophical work, or any other text that resonates with your beliefs and spiritual path. The key is to select a book that holds wisdom and insights that you seek to access.

2. Cleansing and Connection: Before beginning a bibliomancy session, it is advisable to cleanse and consecrate the book to clear any previous energies and establish a sacred connection. You can do this by smudging the book with sacred herbs, passing it through incense smoke, or using other purifying rituals. This process helps to create a focused and energetically aligned space for the divination practice.

3. Grounding and Centering: Ground yourself by taking a few deep breaths and centering your focus on the present moment. This allows you to quiet your mind and establish a receptive state for receiving guidance from the book.

4. Question or Intention: Formulate a clear question or intention that you wish to seek guidance on. It can be specific or open-ended, depending on what you seek to understand or explore. Hold the question in your mind as you prepare to open the book.

5. Random Page Selection: Open the book to a random page. You can do this by closing your eyes and intuitively flipping through the pages until you feel guided to stop. Alternatively, you can use a specific method, such as running your finger along the edges of the pages until it feels right to stop.

6. Passage Interpretation: Read the passage or text that your eyes fall upon and contemplate its meaning in relation to your question or intention. Pay attention to the words, phrases, or sentences that stand out to you and consider how they may offer guidance or insight. Reflect on the symbolism, imagery, and overall message conveyed by the passage.

7. Intuition and Personal Connection: Allow your intuition to guide the interpretation of the passage. Trust your inner knowing and the intuitive impressions that arise as you read. Consider how the words resonate with your personal experiences, beliefs, and emotions. Often, the in-

sights gained through bibliomancy are deeply personal and tailored to your unique situation.

8. Symbolic and Synchronistic Meanings: In addition to the literal interpretation of the passage, be open to symbolic and synchronistic meanings that may emerge. Notice any patterns, themes, or connections between the words or concepts in the passage and your question or current circumstances. These synchronicities can provide additional layers of meaning and guidance.

9. Reflection and Application: After the bibliomancy session, take time to reflect on the insights gained. Consider how the guidance offered by the book aligns with your own intuition and resonates with your personal journey. Contemplate how you can apply the wisdom received to make informed decisions, gain clarity, or navigate challenges in your life.

10. Practice and Experimentation: Bibliomancy, like any form of divination, becomes more potent with practice and experimentation. Explore different books, passages, or techniques to expand your understanding and connection with the practice. Maintain a journal to record the questions, passages, and interpretations to track patterns, progress, and personal growth.

Bibliomancy in witchcraft divination provides a sacred and insightful way to tap into the wisdom of written words and engage in a dialogue with the spiritual realm. Through this practice, witches can access guidance, gain new perspectives, and deepen their connection to the texts that hold spiritual significance for them.

Feather Divination:: Feather divination, also known as ornithomancy or alectromancy, is a form of divination in witchcraft that involves interpreting the messages and omens carried by feathers. Feathers have long been regarded as sacred symbols and are believed to hold spiritual energy and messages from the spiritual realm.

1. Feather Selection: To practice feather divination, start by collecting feathers from various sources such as birds you find in nature, bird sanctuaries, or even from reputable suppliers. It's important to ensure that the feathers are obtained ethically and legally, without causing harm to birds or violating any local regulations.

2. Cleansing and Preparation: Before using a feather for divination, it's essential to cleanse it energetically to remove any residual energies it may carry. You can do this by smudging the feather with sage, palo santo, or another cleansing herb. Alternatively, you can pass it through the smoke of incense or hold it under running water while visualizing any negative energies being washed away.

3. Connection and Intention: Set a clear intention for your feather divination practice. Focus on what specific guidance or insights you seek from the feathers. This intention helps establish a strong connection with the spiritual realm and attracts the appropriate energies and messages.

4. Interpretation: Feather divination can be approached in several ways, depending on your personal preference and intuitive guidance. Here are a few common methods:

a. Feather Symbols: Observe the color, shape, and size of the feather. Each of these attributes may carry symbolic meaning. For example, a black feather can symbolize protection or transformation, while a white feather can represent purity or spiritual guidance. Consider the feather's overall appearance and any personal associations you have with its symbolism.

b. Feather Placement: Pay attention to where you find the feather and its position relative to your path or surroundings. Feathers discovered in unusual or unexpected places may hold particular significance. Additionally, the direction the feather points when you find it can offer further clues or indications.

c. Feather Messages: Connect with your intuition and listen to the messages that come to you as you hold or observe the feather. These messages can be visual, auditory, or intuitive impressions. Trust your inner guidance and interpret the messages in a way that feels authentic and resonates with your intuition.

d. Feather Rituals: You can incorporate feather divination into rituals or meditation practices. Hold the feather in your hand or place it on your altar, and focus your thoughts and intentions on receiving guidance. Visualize the energy of the feather merging with your own energy, opening a channel for divine communication.

1. Journaling and Reflection: It's helpful to keep a journal dedicated to your feather divination practice. Record the feathers you come across, their attributes, the circumstances of their discovery, and any intuitive messages or insights you receive. Over time, patterns may emerge, providing a deeper understanding of the messages and symbolism associated with feathers.

2. Ethical Considerations: As with any divinatory practice, it's important to approach feather divination with respect and ethical considerations. Ensure that the feathers you use are legally obtained and do not harm birds or disrupt their natural habitats. Treat the feathers as sacred objects and handle them with care and reverence.

3. Integration and Action: After a feather divination session, take time to reflect on the messages and insights received. Consider how they relate to your current circumstances, challenges, or goals. Determine practical steps you can take to incorporate the guidance into your life and manifest positive changes or growth.

Feather divination in witchcraft provides a powerful and intuitive way to connect with the spiritual realm and receive guidance. Through observation, interpretation, and deep listening, witches can tap into the wisdom and messages carried by feathers, gaining insights and aligning themselves with the energies of the natural world.

Ogham Divination: Ogham divination, also known as Ogham staves or Ogham oracle, is a form of divination that utilizes the ancient Celtic Ogham alphabet for guidance and insight. Ogham is an ancient script consisting of a series of lines or notches carved onto wooden staves, stones, or other objects. Here is an extensive description of Ogham divination in witchcraft:

1. Ogham Alphabet: The Ogham alphabet consists of a series of 20 characters or symbols, each representing a specific letter and associated with a particular tree or plant. The characters are composed of straight or diagonal lines intersecting a central line known as the "fid" or "twig." Each Ogham symbol is linked to specific qualities, energies, and correspondences.

2. Ogham Staves: Ogham staves are typically long, slender pieces of wood or rods, traditionally made from the corresponding trees associated with each Ogham symbol. However, modern Ogham staves can be made from other materials, such as bone, stone, or metal. Each stave is marked with the appropriate Ogham symbol, usually carved or painted onto the surface.

3. Casting and Selection: To perform Ogham divination, the practitioner casts or scatters the Ogham staves onto a surface, such as a cloth or a designated Ogham divination board. Alternatively, the staves can be placed in a bag or container, and a specific number is drawn or chosen randomly. The selection process can vary depending on personal preference and the diviner's intuitive guidance.

4. Interpretation: Once the staves have been cast or selected, the diviner interprets the Ogham symbols and their arrangement. The interpretation can be based on various factors, including the position of the staves, the orientation of the symbols, and any intuitive impressions or feelings that arise during the process.

5. Ogham Meanings: Each Ogham symbol carries its own meanings and associations. These meanings are often derived from the corresponding tree or plant, as well as from ancient Celtic lore, symbolism, and the diviner's personal understanding. For example, the Ogham symbol "Fearn" represents the Alder tree and is associated with protection, transformation, and intuitive guidance.

6. Intuition and Insight: Ogham divination relies on the diviner's intuition and ability to tap into their own inner wisdom. As the diviner explores the meanings of the Ogham symbols, they also consider their intuitive impressions and any additional insights or messages that arise during the reading. This intuitive element adds depth and personalization to the divination process.

7. Ogham Spreads: Similar to other divination systems, Ogham divination can incorporate various spreads or layouts to provide more detailed information and guidance. Some popular Ogham spreads include the single-stave draw for quick answers or daily guidance, the three-stave spread for past, present, and future insights, and the nine-stave grid for a comprehensive overview.

8. Study and Practice: Ogham divination requires study and practice to become proficient. Learning about the individual Ogham symbols, their correspondences, and the associated tree or plant lore enhances the diviner's understanding and ability to interpret the messages accurately. Regular practice and reflection help deepen the connection with the Ogham symbols and refine the diviner's skills over time.

9. Integration and Application: After a reading, it is important to reflect on the messages received and consider how they relate to your current situation or question. Determine how you can integrate the guidance into your life, make informed decisions, or work with the energies represented by the Ogham symbols. Acting based on the insights gained from Ogham divination can help manifest positive changes and spiritual growth.

Ogham divination in witchcraft offers a unique and ancient method of seeking guidance and connecting with the wisdom of the natural world. Through the symbols and energies of the Ogham alphabet, practitioners can gain insights, receive guidance, and deepen their connection to the Celtic spiritual traditions.

Cloud Scrying: Cloud scrying is a form of divination in witchcraft that involves observing and interpreting the shapes, patterns, and movements of clouds to gain insights and receive messages from the spiritual realm. It is a practice deeply connected to nature and the elements, allowing witches to tap into the wisdom and symbolism of the sky. Here is an extensive description of cloud scrying in witchcraft divination:

1. Preparation: Find a quiet and comfortable outdoor space where you can have an unobstructed view of the sky. Choose a time when the sky is relatively clear with scattered or puffy clouds, as they tend to be more conducive to cloud scrying. Ground yourself by taking a few deep breaths, centering your focus, and setting your intention to receive guidance and insights through cloud scrying.

2. Observation: Gaze up at the sky and allow your eyes to soften as you take in the expanse of clouds. Observe the shapes, colors, and movements of the clouds. Notice if there are any patterns, distinct formations, or changes occurring. Pay attention to the overall atmosphere and energy of the sky.

3. Relaxation and Receptivity: Relax your mind and let go of any expectations or preconceived notions. Enter into a state of receptivity and open yourself to the messages that the clouds may reveal. Allow your intuition to guide you as you interpret the images and symbols that emerge.

4. Interpretation: Cloud scrying is highly subjective and personal, as the interpretations of the cloud formations depend on the individual's unique perspective and intuitive insights. As you observe the clouds, consider the symbolism and meaning associated with the shapes and patterns you perceive. For example, a heart-shaped cloud may symbolize love or emotional connection, while a swirling vortex may indicate a time of transition or change.

5. Free Association: Engage in free association as you interpret the cloud formations. Let your mind wander and make connections between the shapes you see and various aspects of your life or the questions you seek answers to. Notice any emotions, memories, or intuitive impressions that arise as you engage with the clouds.

6. Record Keeping: Keep a journal dedicated to cloud scrying, where you can document your observations, interpretations, and any messages or insights received. Write down the date, time, location, and weather conditions during your cloud scrying session. Include sketches or descriptions of the cloud formations that stood out to you, as well as any thoughts or feelings that accompanied them.

7. Symbolic Associations: Develop your own symbolic associations based on personal experiences, cultural references, or the folklore and mythology of clouds. For example, in some traditions, dark and stormy clouds may represent challenges or upheaval, while fluffy and serene clouds may signify peace or harmony.

8. Meditation and Reflection: After a cloud scrying session, take time to

meditate and reflect on the messages and insights you received. Consider how the cloud formations relate to your current circumstances, questions, or intentions. Contemplate the guidance and guidance the clouds offered and how you can apply it in your life.

9. Practice and Patience: Cloud scrying is a skill that improves with practice and patience. The more you engage in this form of divination, the better you become at recognizing patterns, understanding symbolism, and interpreting the messages presented by the clouds. Allow yourself time to develop your skills and trust in your intuitive abilities.

Cloud scrying in witchcraft divination offers a beautiful and accessible way to connect with the natural world and receive guidance from the spiritual realm. By engaging with the ever-changing canvas of the sky, witches can tap into the wisdom, symbolism, and energies of the clouds, gaining insights, and deepening their spiritual connection.

Aura Reading: Aura reading is a form of divination in witchcraft that involves perceiving and interpreting the energy field that surrounds living beings, known as the aura. The aura is believed to contain information about a person's physical, emotional, and spiritual state. Aura reading enables witches to gain insight into the energetic aspects of individuals and tap into the subtle energies surrounding them.

1. Preparation: Find a quiet and comfortable space where you can focus without distractions. It's helpful to have good lighting and a neutral background against which the person's aura can be seen more easily. Ground yourself by taking a few deep breaths, centering your focus, and setting your intention to read and interpret the aura accurately and ethically.

2. Sensory Perception: To read a person's aura, begin by softening your gaze

and shifting your focus slightly beyond their physical body. Relax your eyes and let them defocus, allowing your peripheral vision to come into play. With practice, you may start to perceive subtle colors, shapes, or vibrations around the person.

3. Color Interpretation: Pay attention to the colors you perceive within the aura. Different colors have different meanings and can indicate various aspects of a person's energy and state of being. For example, blue might represent calmness and communication, while red can indicate passion and energy. Trust your intuition and any associations or feelings that arise when perceiving specific colors.

4. Shape and Density: Notice the shape and density of the aura. Some individuals may have a defined, compact aura, while others may have a more expansive and diffuse one. The shape and density can provide insights into the person's personality traits, emotional state, or spiritual energy. Experiment with different ways of perceiving and interpreting these aspects.

5. Energy Sensations: As you focus on the person's aura, pay attention to any physical or energetic sensations you may experience. Some witches report tingling, warmth, coolness, or subtle vibrations when reading auras. These sensations can provide additional information or validation of the impressions you receive.

6. Intuitive Impressions: Aura reading is an intuitive practice. Allow yourself to receive intuitive impressions, feelings, or messages that come to you as you observe the aura. Trust your intuition and any guidance or insights that arise during the reading. Remember, the interpretation of the aura is subjective, and your intuition plays a vital role in understanding its meaning.

7. Ethical Considerations: Respect the privacy and consent of the indi-

vidual whose aura you are reading. Always seek their permission before conducting an aura reading and explain the purpose and nature of the practice. Practice aura reading with integrity and empathy, focusing on providing guidance and support rather than intruding or judging.

8. Practice and Reflection: Aura reading requires practice to refine your skills and interpretations. Engage in regular aura reading sessions to develop your abilities. Keep a journal to record your observations, impressions, and interpretations. Reflect on your experiences, noting any patterns or insights that emerge over time.

9. Integration and Communication: After an aura reading, communicate your observations and interpretations to the individual if they have requested a reading or if you have their consent. Provide the information with sensitivity and openness, emphasizing that the interpretation is subjective and offering suggestions or insights for their personal growth and well-being.

Aura reading in witchcraft divination offers a valuable tool for witches to connect with the energetic aspects of individuals. Through the interpretation of colors, shapes, and energy sensations, aura reading allows witches to gain insight into the physical, emotional, and spiritual aspects of a person's being, supporting their journey of self-discovery and spiritual growth.

Mirror Divination: Mirror divination, also known as scrying or mirror gazing, is a form of divination in witchcraft that involves using a reflective surface, such as a mirror, to gain insight and receive messages from the spiritual realm. It is a practice that allows witches to tap into their intuition and access hidden knowledge.

Preparation: Find a quiet and dimly lit space where you can sit comfortably in front of a mirror. Ensure that the mirror is clean and free from any distractions or reflections that may interfere with your focus. Settle yourself by taking a few deep breaths, centering your mind, and setting your intention to receive guidance and insights through mirror divination.

1. Focus and Relaxation: Gaze into the mirror without straining your eyes or fixating too intensely. Soften your gaze and allow your vision to blur slightly. Relax your mind and body, releasing any thoughts or distractions. Enter into a state of receptivity and openness, inviting the messages and images to come forth.

2. Scrying Techniques: There are various techniques you can use during mirror divination. One common technique is to focus on a specific point in the mirror and allow images or impressions to form around it. Another technique involves letting your gaze wander across the mirror's surface, allowing the shapes and patterns to emerge naturally.

3. Symbolic Interpretation: As you gaze into the mirror, pay attention to any images, symbols, or scenes that appear. These may be literal or metaphorical representations that hold significance for your situation or question. Trust your intuition and any associations, emotions, or impressions that arise as you engage with the images.

4. Emotional and Energetic Sensations: Notice any emotional or energetic sensations you experience during the mirror divination. You may feel shifts in energy, vibrations, tingling, or other subtle sensations. These sensations can provide additional insights and serve as validation for the messages or images you receive.

5. Personal Symbolism: Develop your own personal symbolism and associations during mirror divination. Certain symbols or images may hold specific meanings for you based on your experiences, cultural background, or spiritual beliefs. Reflect on the symbolism that resonates with you and consider how it relates to the guidance you receive.

6. Interpretation and Reflection: After your mirror divination session, take time to reflect on the images, symbols, and impressions you received. Consider how they relate to your current situation, questions, or intentions. Engage in introspection and journaling to further explore the insights and guidance provided through the mirror divination.

7. Practice and Patience: Mirror divination is a skill that improves with practice and patience. The more you engage in this form of divination, the more you develop your ability to interpret the messages and symbolism within the mirror. Trust the process and allow yourself to grow in confidence and proficiency over time.

8. Integration and Action: Mirror divination is not just about receiving guidance; it also involves integrating that guidance into your life. Consider how the insights you gained through mirror divination can inform your choices, actions, or personal growth. Apply the wisdom received and take steps toward manifesting positive changes based on the messages you received.

Mirror divination in witchcraft is a powerful and mystical practice that allows witches to access hidden knowledge and receive guidance from the spiritual realm. Through the use of a mirror, witches can tap into their intuition, explore symbolism, and connect with deeper aspects of themselves and the universe

These are just a few examples of witch's divination practices. Each witch may have their preferred methods and may combine different techniques based on their personal beliefs and intuitive abilities. Divination allows witches to access hidden knowledge, receive guidance, and deepen their spiritual connection. It is a powerful tool for self-discovery, decision-making, and navigating life's challenges.

Symbols and rituals in witchcraft are highly diverse, and their meanings can vary among practitioners. They serve as powerful tools for focusing intention, channeling energy, and connecting with the spiritual realm. Witches use these symbols and rituals to deepen their spiritual practice, honor nature, and harness their own inner power.

Chapter Twenty-Six

Meditation and Visualization: Inner Journeys in Witchcraft

Meditation and visualization are integral practices for witches, allowing them to deepen their spiritual connection, harness their inner power, and manifest their desires.

Meditation

Meditation is a practice of calming the mind, focusing one's awareness, and achieving a state of deep relaxation. Witches use meditation as a tool for grounding, centering, and quieting the mind to access their inner wisdom and connect with higher realms. Here are the key elements of witch's meditation:

Setting Intentions: Before starting the meditation, witches set their intentions for the practice. This could be gaining clarity, finding peace, receiving guidance, or any other specific purpose.

Creating Sacred Space: Witches often create a sacred space for meditation by cleansing the area, lighting candles or incense, and placing meaningful objects or symbols. This helps to create a peaceful and energetically aligned environment.

Posture and Breath: Witches find a comfortable sitting or lying position and focus on their breath. They take slow, deep breaths, allowing the body to relax and the mind to become more present.

Visualization: Witches may incorporate visualization techniques during meditation, which involves creating mental images or scenes that evoke specific emotions, intentions, or experiences.

Guided Meditation: Witches may use guided meditations, either by listening to pre-recorded guided meditation tracks or by following the instructions of a practitioner or teacher. Guided meditations often incorporate visualization and help guide the practitioner through specific journeys or experiences.

Mantras and Affirmations: Witches may chant mantras or repeat affirmations during meditation to focus the mind, enhance intention, or connect with specific energies.

Mindfulness: Witches practice mindfulness during meditation, observing their thoughts, feelings, and bodily sensations without judgment. This helps to cultivate present-moment awareness and deepen the connection to the self.

Visualization

Visualization is the practice of creating vivid mental images in the mind's eye. Witches use visualization to manifest their desires, connect with deities or spirit guides, and explore the spiritual realms. Here are the key elements of witch's visualization:

Setting Intentions: Before beginning the visualization practice, witches set clear intentions about what they wish to achieve or experience through visualization.

Relaxation and Focus: Witches relax their bodies and minds through deep breathing and relaxation techniques. They then focus their attention on the specific visualization they wish to create.

Imagination and Sensory Details: Witches engage their imagination, bringing the desired images to life with vivid sensory details. They visualize colors, textures, sounds, scents, and emotions associated with their intention.

Symbolism and Archetypes: Witches may incorporate symbolism and archetypal images in their visualizations to tap into the collective unconscious and access deeper layers of meaning and wisdom.

Energy and Intention: Witches infuse their visualizations with their intention and energy, believing that their focused thoughts and emotions can manifest in the physical world.

Integration and Reflection: After the visualization, witches take time to integrate the experience and reflect on any insights, messages, or feelings that arose during the practice.

Regular Practice: Witches engage in regular meditation and visualization practices to enhance their skills, deepen their connection to the spiritual realms, and align their energies with their intentions.

Both meditation and visualization are powerful tools for witches to cultivate self-awareness, expand consciousness, and connect with the energies and forces of the universe. Through these practices, witches can tap into their inner wisdom, enhance their magical abilities, and manifest positive change in their lives and the world around them.

Chapter Twenty-Seven

Male Witches: Breaking Stereotypes and Embracing Diversity

Male witches, also known as warlocks or wizards, play a significant role in the history and practice of witchcraft.

Historical Perspective: Throughout history, male witches have been present in various cultures and societies. While witchcraft has often been associated with women, men have also practiced witchcraft and held positions of power within magical traditions.

Magical Practices: Male witches engage in the same magical practices as their female counterparts. They may perform rituals, spells, divination, and other forms of magic to connect with the spiritual realm, harness energy, and manifest their intentions. Male witches draw upon their own unique experiences, perspectives, and energies in their magical work.

Traditions and Paths: Male witches may follow specific traditions or paths within witchcraft, such as Wicca, Druidry, or Hermeticism, or they may create their own unique practices. They may choose to work solitary or within groups, participating in rituals and ceremonies alongside other practitioners.

Diversity: Male witches, like female witches, come from diverse backgrounds and cultures. They may have different spiritual beliefs, cultural influences, and practices within witchcraft. Male witches can be found in various countries, representing different ethnicities, sexual orientations, and genders.

Stereotypes and Misconceptions: Male witches have often faced stereotypes and misconceptions, as witchcraft has historically been associated with women. Some portrayals in media and literature have perpetuated negative or inaccurate stereotypes, but it is essential to recognize that male witches are diverse individuals with their own unique experiences and practices.

Role in Covens and Groups: Male witches can play important roles in covens and magical groups. They may act as leaders, teachers, ritual facilitators, or contributors to the group's collective energy. Male witches bring their unique perspectives and energies to group dynamics and contribute to the overall spiritual growth and well-being of the community.

Gender Equality: In modern witchcraft, there is a growing emphasis on gender equality and inclusivity. Many practitioners strive to challenge and dismantle gender-based stereotypes and hierarchies within witchcraft. This includes recognizing the valuable contributions and perspectives of male witches and creating spaces that are welcoming and supportive for practitioners of all genders.

Personal Empowerment: Male witches, like all witches, seek personal empowerment and spiritual growth through their practice. They work to develop their magical skills, deepen their connection with the divine, and cultivate their personal power and intuition. Male witches embrace their own unique strengths, talents, and energies in their spiritual journeys.

We must begin to recognize that witchcraft is an inclusive and diverse practice that welcomes individuals of all genders. Male witches contribute to the rich history of witchcraft, bringing their own unique experiences, energies, and perspectives to the craft. Like their female counterparts, male witches play a vital role in the exploration, preservation, and evolution of witchcraft traditions and practices.

Chapter Twenty-Eight

Wicca: A Comprehensive Exploration of the Modern Witchcraft Religion

Wicca is a modern pagan religious movement that emerged in the mid-20th century. It is a nature-based spirituality that draws inspiration from various pre-Christian and folk traditions. Here is an extensive description of Wicca, including its history and present-day practices

History of Wicca: Wicca was founded in the early 1950s by Gerald Gardner, a British civil servant and amateur anthropologist. Gardner claimed to have been initiated into a secret coven of witches in England and sought to revive and reconstruct ancient pagan practices. He published several books, including "Witchcraft Today" and "The Meaning of Witchcraft," which brought attention to the religion and its practices.

Wicca drew influence from various sources, including folklore, ceremonial magic, Freemasonry, and Western esoteric traditions. Gardner incorporated ritual tools, such as the athame (ritual knife) and chalice and celebrated the cycles of the moon and seasonal festivals known as Sabbats.

Wicca's Influence and Development: After Gardner's work, Wicca experienced a period of growth and expansion, particularly in the United Kingdom and the United States. Many practitioners developed their own variations and traditions within Wicca, leading to the emergence of diverse branches and lineages. Notable figures such as Doreen Valiente, Raymond Buckland, and Starhawk played significant roles in shaping Wicca's development and introducing new concepts and practices.

Core Beliefs and Practices: While there is no centralized authority in Wicca, and beliefs and practices can vary among individuals and traditions, there are some core beliefs and practices that are commonly shared. Here is an extensive description of the Wiccan core beliefs and practices:

1. **Polytheistic Nature-Based Spirituality**: Wiccans believe in a polytheistic worldview, honoring and worshiping multiple deities. The most revered deities are a God and Goddess, representing the divine masculine and feminine energies. These deities are often associated with nature and its cycles.

1. **The Wiccan Rede**: The Wiccan Rede is a moral guideline that states, "An it harm none, do what ye will." It encourages Wiccans to act responsibly, considering the potential consequences of their actions and striving to avoid causing harm to themselves, others, and the natural world.

1. **The Law of Threefold Return**: Wiccans believe in the concept of karma, which is often expressed through the Law of Threefold Return. This law suggests that whatever energy or actions one puts out into the world, whether positive or negative, will return to them threefold. It emphasizes personal responsibility and the importance of ethical behavior.

1. **Ritual and Magick**:(Wiccans add a "k" to the word Magic) Wiccans practice rituals and magick to connect with the divine, harness natural energies, and manifest desired outcomes. Rituals often involve the casting of circles, calling upon deities, the use of tools such as the athame (ritual knife) and chalice, and the performance of spells, divination, and meditation.

1. **Wheel of the Year**: Wiccans celebrate a series of seasonal festivals known as the Wheel of the Year, which mark significant points in the agricultural and astronomical calendar. These include the solstices, equinoxes, and cross-quarter days. Each festival is an opportunity to honor the cycles of nature, express gratitude, and align with the energy of the season.

1. **Elemental Associations**: Wicca recognizes the importance of the elements—earth, air, fire, water, and sometimes spirit—as fundamental forces in the universe. Each element is associated with specific qualities, directions, and correspondences. Wiccans may work with these elements in rituals, spells, and magickal workings.

1. **Sacred Space and Altar**: Wiccans often create and maintain sacred spaces for rituals and spiritual practices. This can include the casting of a circle, the creation of an altar, and the arrangement of symbolic items

representing the elements, deities, and personal intentions. The altar serves as a focal point for connecting with the divine and conducting magickal workings.

1. **Book of Shadows**: Wiccans typically keep a personal Book of Shadows, which is a journal or grimoire that records their spiritual experiences, rituals, spells, correspondences, and insights. It serves as a personal guide, containing accumulated wisdom and knowledge that can be passed down through generations.

1. **Ancestor and Nature Reverence**: Wiccans often hold deep reverence for their ancestors and the natural world. They recognize the interconnectedness of all beings and honor the wisdom and guidance of their lineage and the spirits of nature. Wiccans may engage in practices such as ancestor veneration and environmental stewardship.

1. **Personal Growth and Empowerment**: Wiccans value personal growth, self-discovery, and empowerment. They see their spiritual path as a journey of continuous learning and transformation. Wiccans often engage in practices that promote self-awareness, self-care, and the development of psychic and intuitive abilities.

It's important to note that these descriptions provide a general overview of Wiccan beliefs and practices, and individual interpretations and practices may vary. Wicca is a diverse and inclusive spiritual path that encourages personal exploration, connection with nature, and the pursuit of spiritual harmony and balance.

Wiccans celebrate eight Sabbats, which are seasonal festivals that mark significant points in the solar and agricultural calendar. These include Samhain (October 31), Yule (Winter Solstice), Imbolc (February 2), Ostara (Spring Equinox), Beltane (May 1), Litha (Summer Solstice), Lammas (August 1), and Mabon (Autumn Equinox). Esbats, monthly rituals held during the full moon, are also observed to honor the lunar cycles.

Ethics and Principles: Wicca is a religion that emphasizes ethical behavior and personal responsibility. While there is no central authority in Wicca, there are common ethical principles and guidelines that many Wiccans adhere to. Here is an extensive description of the Wiccan ethics and principles:

1. **The Wiccan Rede:** The Wiccan Rede is a moral guideline that is often summed up as "An it harm none, do what ye will." This principle encourages Wiccans to act responsibly, considering the potential consequences of their actions and striving to avoid causing harm to themselves, others, and the natural world. It emphasizes the importance of free will, personal choice, and taking responsibility for the consequences of one's actions.

1. **Law of Threefold Return**: The Law of Threefold Return is a belief that the energy or actions one puts out into the world, whether positive or negative, will return to them threefold. It is a concept of karma and encourages Wiccans to consider the ethical implications of their actions and to strive for harmony and balance in their interactions with others.

1. **Respect for Nature**: Wiccans hold a deep reverence for nature and strive to live in harmony with the natural world. They recognize the interconnectedness of all living beings and the importance of environmental stewardship. Wiccans often engage in practices that honor and

protect the Earth, such as sustainable living, conservation efforts, and supporting environmental causes.

1. **Personal Responsibility**: Wicca places a strong emphasis on personal responsibility. Wiccans are encouraged to take ownership of their thoughts, words, and actions. They understand that they have the power to shape their own lives and the responsibility to make ethical choices that align with their values and beliefs.

1. **Consent and Boundaries**: Wiccans value consent and respect for personal boundaries. They understand the importance of seeking permission and obtaining informed consent before engaging in any magickal or ritual practices involving others. This principle extends to all aspects of life, emphasizing the importance of respecting personal autonomy and boundaries.

1. **Honesty and Integrity**: Wiccans value honesty and integrity in their interactions with others. They strive to be truthful, both with themselves and with others. Wiccans recognize that honesty builds trust and fosters healthy relationships.

1. **Non-Discrimination and Inclusivity**: Wicca promotes inclusivity and non-discrimination. Wiccans respect and honor diversity, recognizing that all individuals have inherent worth and dignity regardless of their race, ethnicity, gender, sexual orientation, or religious background. Wiccans reject discrimination and prejudice and strive to create inclusive and accepting communities.

1. **Balance and Harmony:** Wiccans seek balance and harmony in their lives. They recognize the importance of maintaining equilibrium between various aspects of life, such as work and personal life, spirituality and mundane responsibilities, and the pursuit of personal desires and the needs of others. Wiccans aim to create a sense of balance and harmony within themselves and in their relationships with others.

1. **Personal Growth and Self-Awareness:** Wicca encourages personal growth and self-awareness. Wiccans engage in practices that promote self-reflection, introspection, and the development of self-awareness. They strive to continuously learn and grow spiritually, emotionally, and intellectually.

1. **Community and Service**: Wiccans value community and service. They often come together in covens or other groups to support and learn from one another. Wiccans may engage in acts of service and contribute to the well-being of their communities through volunteering, charitable work, and supporting social justice causes.

These principles form a foundation for ethical behavior in Wicca, but it is important to note that individual interpretations and practices may vary. Wiccans are encouraged to reflect on these principles and apply them in a way that aligns with their own beliefs and values.

Wicca Today: Wicca continues to be a recognized and practiced religion in many parts of the world. Here is a description of the present-day status of Wicca:

1. **Legal Recognition**: Wicca and other forms of modern witchcraft have gained legal recognition in various countries. While the level of recog-

nition varies, many countries, including the United States, Canada, and the United Kingdom, recognize Wicca as a legitimate religion and grant it legal protections and rights.

Growing Popularity:

Wicca has seen a significant increase in popularity over the past few decades. Many people are drawn to its nature-based spirituality, focus on personal empowerment, and celebration of diversity and inclusivity. Wiccan books, websites, and social media platforms have made information more accessible, contributing to the growth of Wiccan communities and the spread of knowledge.

1. **Diverse Practices**: Wicca encompasses a broad range of practices and traditions, allowing individuals to adapt and personalize their spiritual path. There are numerous Wiccan traditions, such as Gardnerian, Alexandrian, Dianic, and eclectic Wicca. Some practitioners follow specific lineages, while others create their own unique blend of practices.

1. **Online Communities and Resources**: The internet has played a significant role in connecting Wiccans worldwide. Online communities and forums provide platforms for sharing knowledge, discussing experiences, and offering support. Many websites, blogs, and social media accounts are dedicated to Wiccan teachings, rituals, and resources.

1. **Wiccan Festivals and Gatherings**: Wiccan festivals and gatherings, known as "Pagan Pride" events or "Witch camps," are organized in many countries. These events offer opportunities for Wiccans and other pagan practitioners to come together, celebrate the seasonal festivals, share

knowledge, and build community.

1. **Interfaith Dialogue**: Wicca has actively participated in interfaith dialogue and collaborations with other religious groups. Wiccan representatives have been involved in interfaith organizations, conferences, and initiatives to promote understanding, respect, and religious freedom for all.

1. **Environmental and Social Activism**: Many Wiccans are committed to environmental stewardship and social justice. They engage in activism, participate in ecological preservation projects, and support causes related to human rights, LGBTQ+ rights, racial justice, and women's empowerment.

1. **Legal Challenges and Discrimination**: Despite gaining legal recognition in many countries, Wiccans may still face challenges and discrimination. Instances of religious intolerance, prejudice, and misunderstanding can occur at individual, community, or institutional levels. Efforts are ongoing to promote understanding, dispel myths, and advocate for religious freedom and equality.

1. **Wiccan Clergy and Ritual Services**: Wiccan clergy, such as High Priests and High Priestesses, perform religious ceremonies, rituals, and rites of passage within Wiccan communities. They may officiate weddings, conduct handfasting's (Wiccan commitment ceremonies), and facilitate other rites and rituals.

1. **Integration into Mainstream Society**: Wicca has gradually gained

acceptance and visibility in mainstream society. Books, movies, television shows, and other media have portrayed Wiccan characters and themes, contributing to a better understanding and representation of the religion.

It's important to note that the status of Wicca can vary by region and individual circumstances. While progress has been made in terms of recognition and acceptance, challenges and misconceptions may still exist. The present-day status of Wicca is dynamic and influenced by social, cultural, and legal factors.

Chapter Twenty-Nine

Green Witches: Nature-Centric Practices and Eco-Spirituality

Green Witchcraft is a contemporary form of witchcraft that focuses on the natural world, herbalism, and the balance between humans and nature. Green witches, also known as garden witches or nature witches, have a deep connection to the Earth and draw their spiritual and magical practices from nature-based traditions.

Here are some key aspects of Green Witchcraft:

Nature Connection:

Green witches have an intrinsic and profound connection with nature that is deeply rooted in their spiritual and magical practices. They view the natural world as a sacred entity, and their beliefs and actions reflect a reverence for the Earth and all its living beings.

1. **Deep Respect for Nature**: Green witches hold a deep respect for the natural world and acknowledge that everything in it is interconnected. They recognize the inherent value and worth of every living creature, plant, and element of the Earth. This respect guides their actions, and they strive to live in harmony with nature rather than exploiting or dominating it.

1. **Nature as a Teacher**: Green witches see nature as a wise and knowledgeable teacher. They observe the cycles of the seasons, the behavior of animals, and the growth of plants to gain insights into the larger patterns of life. They understand that nature has its own rhythms and lessons to teach, and they strive to learn from these teachings to enhance their own spiritual growth.

1. **Ecological Consciousness**: Green witches are deeply concerned about the well-being and preservation of the Earth. They recognize the impact that human actions have on the environment and work actively to promote ecological consciousness and sustainable living. They advocate for conservation, recycling, and reducing waste, and they often participate in environmental activism to protect natural habitats and promote the health of ecosystems.

1. **Herbalism and Plant Magic**: Green witches have a strong affinity for plants and their healing properties. They study herbalism and work with plants for medicinal, magical, and spiritual purposes. They have extensive knowledge of different herbs, their properties, and how to cultivate and use them. Green witches often create herbal remedies, teas, potions, and incenses, harnessing the power and wisdom of plants to

support physical and emotional well-being.

1. **Nature-Based Rituals and Ceremonies**: Green witches frequently incorporate nature-based rituals and ceremonies into their spiritual practice. They celebrate the cycles of the seasons, such as solstices and equinoxes, and honor the natural elements such as earth, air, fire, and water. These rituals may involve meditation in natural settings, offering gratitude to the land and its creatures, or performing ceremonies to mark significant life events or rites of passage.

1. **Connection with Elemental Energies**: Green witches recognize and work with the energies of the natural elements: earth, air, fire, and water. They understand that each element holds its own unique qualities and symbolism, and they use these energies in their rituals, spells, and magical workings. They may invoke the elemental energies for balance, protection, purification, or manifestation.

1. **Communing with Spirits and Deities of Nature**: Green witches often establish connections and form relationships with spirits and deities associated with nature. They believe in the existence of nature spirits, faeries, and other elemental beings, and they may communicate and work with them for guidance, protection, and assistance in their magical endeavors. Some green witches also honor and invoke ancient deities that embody nature's energies and qualities.

1. **Nature Walks and Meditation**: Green witches regularly engage in nature walks and meditative practices to deepen their connection with the Earth. They seek solace and inspiration in natural settings, immersing themselves in the beauty and tranquility of forests, meadows, moun-

tains, or bodies of water. They practice mindfulness, connecting with the sights, sounds, and sensations of nature, and find inner peace and spiritual nourishment through these experiences.

The nature connection of Green Witches is all-encompassing and influences every aspect of their lives. They honor and protect the Earth, seek wisdom from the natural world, work with plants and elemental energies, perform rituals in natural settings, and find spiritual solace in the beauty of nature.

Herbalism and Plant Magic:

Green witches have a strong affinity for herbalism and plant magic, which are central aspects of their spiritual and magical practices. They recognize the healing properties, energetic qualities, and spiritual wisdom that plants hold, and they work with them in many ways. Here is an extensive description of green witches' herbalism and plant magic:

1. **Study of Plants**: Green witches dedicate themselves to studying plants in-depth. They develop a comprehensive knowledge of various herbs, flowers, trees, and other botanicals, including their physical characteristics, medicinal properties, folklore, and magical associations. They understand the parts of plants, such as leaves, flowers, stems, roots, and seeds, and how each part can be utilized for different purposes.

Medicinal Herbalism: Green witches have a deep understanding of the medicinal properties of plants. They know how to prepare herbal remedies, such as tinctures, teas, salves, and poultices, to support physical and emotional well-being. They use their knowledge of plants' healing properties to address common ailments, boost the immune system, relieve stress, and promote overall health.

Green witches may also incorporate folk remedies and traditional healing practices into their herbalism.

1. **Magical Properties**: Green witches believe that plants possess magical properties and energies that can be harnessed for spellwork and rituals. They understand that different plants have unique correspondences and associations with specific intentions or magical goals. For example, lavender may be used for relaxation and sleep, while rosemary can be used for purification and clarity. Green witches incorporate these correspondences into their magical workings, selecting specific plants or creating herbal blends to enhance their spells, rituals, and intentions.

1. **Plant Spirit Communication**: Green witches develop relationships with the spirits of plants. They believe that each plant has its own consciousness and spirit, and they seek to connect with and learn from these spirits. Through meditation, visualization, and deep observation, green witches can commune with the spirit of a plant, receiving guidance, insights, and teachings. They may ask for permission and offer gratitude when harvesting or working with a plant, fostering a respectful and reciprocal relationship.

1. **Gardening and Plant Cultivation**: Green witches often engage in gardening and plant cultivation as part of their practice. They may have their own herb gardens or indoor plant collections, carefully tending to the needs of the plants they work with. Green witches understand the importance of sustainable and ethical gardening practices, such as organic cultivation, companion planting, and honoring the cycles of growth and harvest. They may also incorporate lunar and seasonal influences into their gardening activities.

1. **Ritual and Sacred Space Decoration**: Green witches use plants to create sacred spaces and altar decorations for rituals and spellcasting. They may gather fresh flowers, herbs, or branches to create floral arrangements, wreaths, or herb bundles that align with the specific energies or intentions of their practice. Green witches understand the power of scent, color, and symbolism in enhancing the magical atmosphere of their sacred spaces.

1. **Plant Divination and Symbolism**: Green witches recognize that plants can be used as tools for divination and symbolism. They may practice methods such as tea leaf reading, flower oracle readings, or using plant-related symbols in their tarot or oracle card interpretations. Green witches also understand the symbolic meanings associated with plants in folklore, mythology, and cultural traditions, and they may incorporate these meanings into their rituals, spells, or magical workings.

1. **Ritual Baths and Cleansing**: Green witches harness the healing and magical properties of plants in ritual baths and cleansing practices. They infuse water with herbs, flowers, or essential oils, creating an herbal bath blend that corresponds to their intentions or needs. These baths are used for physical and spiritual cleansing, relaxation, grounding, or energy purification. Green witches may also create herbal smudge sticks or use herbal-infused waters for space clearing and energetic cleansing.

Green witches deeply engage with herbalism and plant magic, utilizing the healing properties, spiritual energies, and symbolic associations of plants. They study plants extensively, incorporate them into their spell work and rituals, communicate with plant spirits, cultivate gardens, and use plants for divination and cleansing purposes. Their practices honor the wisdom and magic that nature provides through its botanical gifts.

Earth-Centered Spirituality

Earth-centered spirituality lies at the core of the beliefs and practices of green witches. It encompasses a deep reverence for the Earth as a sacred entity and a recognition of the interconnectedness of all living beings. Green witches see the Earth as a source of wisdom, healing, and spiritual nourishment. Here is an extensive description of Earth-centered spirituality with green witches:

1. **Sacredness of the Earth**: Green witches view the Earth as a sacred and living entity deserving of respect, care, and reverence. They recognize that the Earth sustains all life and provides the resources necessary for survival. They understand that every element of the Earth, from the soil and plants to the animals and ecosystems, is interconnected and deserving of protection.

1. **Connection with Nature**: Green witches cultivate a deep and intimate connection with nature. They spend time in natural settings, such as forests, mountains, or bodies of water, to commune with the Earth's energies and find solace and inspiration. They observe and learn from the cycles of the seasons, the behavior of animals, and the growth of plants, seeking wisdom and guidance from these natural processes.

1. **Celebration of the Seasons**: Green witches honor and celebrate the cycles of the seasons as sacred moments of transformation. They mark the solstices, equinoxes, and other seasonal festivals to acknowledge the Earth's changing energies and align themselves with the natural rhythms of life. They may perform rituals, create altars, or participate in com-

munal celebrations to honor and express gratitude for the gifts of each season.

1. **Elemental Connection**: Green witches recognize the presence and significance of the natural elements—earth, air, fire, and water—in their spiritual practice. They understand that each element carries its own energy and symbolism. They work with these elemental energies in rituals, spells, and magical workings, invoking their qualities for balance, protection, manifestation, and spiritual growth.

1. **Ancestor Reverence**: Green witches honor their ancestral connections and recognize the wisdom and guidance that can be gained from those who came before. They acknowledge that their ancestors were intimately connected to the Earth and its cycles, and they seek to carry forward their knowledge and traditions. They may create ancestral altars, perform rituals to honor their lineage, or seek guidance and communication with their ancestors in their spiritual practice.

1. **Sacred Spaces and Altars**: Green witches create sacred spaces and altars dedicated to their Earth-centered spirituality. These spaces serve as focal points for meditation, rituals, and spell work. They often incorporate natural objects, such as stones, feathers, shells, or plants, which represent the Earth and its elements. Green witches infuse their sacred spaces with intention, creating a sanctuary for connection, reflection, and spiritual practice.

1. **Ecological Consciousness**: Green witches are deeply committed to ecological consciousness and sustainable living. They understand the impact of human actions on the Earth and actively work to minimize

their ecological footprint. They promote practices such as recycling, reducing waste, conserving energy, and supporting environmental causes. Green witches often engage in environmental activism, advocating for the preservation of natural habitats and the protection of endangered species.

1. **Healing and Nature-based Remedies**: Green witches recognize the Earth's inherent healing powers and incorporate nature-based remedies into their spiritual and healing practices. They work with herbs, flowers, essential oils, and other natural ingredients to create remedies for physical, emotional, and spiritual ailments. They may utilize herbal teas, tinctures, salves, or aromatherapy to support well-being and promote holistic healing.

Earth-centered spirituality is deeply ingrained in the beliefs and practices of green witches. They hold the Earth as sacred, connect with nature's wisdom, celebrate the cycles of the seasons, work with elemental energies, honor their ancestors, create sacred spaces, and engage in ecological consciousness and healing practices. Through their Earth-centered spirituality, Green Witches seek to cultivate a harmonious and sustainable relationship with the Earth and all its inhabitants.

Rituals and Celebrations

Rituals and celebrations play a significant role in the spiritual practice of green witches. These practices are deeply rooted in their connection with nature, reverence for the Earth, and the cycles of the seasons. Green witches engage in various rituals and celebrations to honor, connect with, and seek guidance from the natural world. Here is an extensive description of rituals and celebrations with green witches:

1. **Sabbats and Equinoxes**: Green witches celebrate the eight sabbats, also known as the Wheel of the Year, which mark the seasonal changes and the turning of the natural cycles. These include Samhain, Yule, Imbolc, Ostara, Beltane, Litha, Lammas, and Mabon. Each sabbat represents a specific point in the agricultural and spiritual year, and green witches often gather to honor these occasions through rituals, feasts, and community celebrations.

1. **Esbats and Moon Magic**: Green witches place a special emphasis on the cycles of the moon and incorporate moon magic into their rituals and practices. Esbats are lunar celebrations that occur at the full and new moons. During these times, green witches gather to work with the lunar energies, perform divination, charge crystals, cast spells, and set intentions aligned with the moon's energy.

1. **Elemental Rituals**: Green witches work with the energies of the four elements—earth, air, fire, and water—and often incorporate elemental rituals into their practice. These rituals involve invoking the elemental energies for specific purposes, such as grounding and stability (earth), inspiration and communication (air), passion and transformation (fire), and emotional healing and intuition (water).

1. **Ancestor Rituals**: Green witches honor their ancestors and connect with their wisdom through ancestor rituals. These rituals may involve setting up ancestral altars, lighting candles, offering food or drink, and speaking words of gratitude and remembrance. Green witches seek guidance, protection, and a deeper connection with their lineage through these rituals.

1. **Plant Magic Rituals**: Green witches engage in rituals specifically focused on plant magic and herbalism. They may gather in nature or their own herb gardens to harvest plants, perform blessings, or create herbal remedies, teas, or incenses. These rituals honor the wisdom and healing properties of plants and seek to harness their magical energies for specific intentions or purposes.

1. **Blessings and Offerings**: Green witches offer blessings and gratitude to the Earth and its inhabitants through various rituals. They may perform land blessings to honor and show respect for the natural world. They also offer prayers, songs, or rituals to show appreciation for the elements, nature spirits, deities, or specific places of power.

1. **Healing Rituals**: Green witches incorporate healing rituals into their practice to support physical, emotional, and spiritual well-being. These rituals may involve energy healing, meditation, visualization, herbal remedies, or sacred baths. Green witches seek to restore balance, promote healing, and cultivate a harmonious connection with the Earth and themselves through these rituals.

1. **Rites of Passage**: Green witches mark significant life events and personal growth through rites of passage rituals. These rituals may include initiations, handfasting's (ritual weddings), baby blessings, or other ceremonies to honor transitions and milestones. They acknowledge the sacredness of these life moments and seek to infuse them with spiritual meaning and connection to the Earth.

1. **Seasonal Crafts and Decorations**: Green witches engage in crafts and

decorate their sacred spaces to reflect the changing seasons and their connection with nature. They create wreaths, floral arrangements, or symbols using natural materials such as leaves, flowers, feathers, or crystals. These crafts and decorations become an integral part of their rituals and celebrations.

1. **Community and Communal Celebrations**: Green witches often come together in community to celebrate and honor the Earth. They may gather in outdoor settings, such as parks or forests, to perform rituals, share food, exchange knowledge, and engage in festivities. These communal celebrations foster a sense of belonging, unity, and support among green witches and their wider spiritual community.

Green witches engage in a variety of rituals and celebrations that are deeply intertwined with their connection to nature, the cycles of the seasons, and their reverence for the Earth. These rituals honor the elements, moon cycles, ancestral wisdom, plants, and other aspects of the natural world. Through these practices, green witches seek spiritual connection, guidance, healing, and a harmonious relationship with the Earth and all its inhabitants.

Environmental Stewardship

Environmental stewardship is a fundamental aspect of the beliefs and practices of green witches. They recognize the importance of caring for and protecting the Earth, understanding that their spiritual well-being is intrinsically connected to the well-being of the natural world. Green witches actively engage in environmental stewardship through various actions and practices. Here is an extensive description of environmental stewardship with green witches:

1. **Sustainable Living**: Green witches strive to live in harmony with the

Earth by adopting sustainable practices in their daily lives. They prioritize reducing waste, conserving energy and water, and practicing mindful consumption. Green witches make conscious choices regarding their food, clothing, and other material possessions, opting for eco-friendly, ethically sourced, and sustainable alternatives whenever possible.

1. **Recycling and Waste Reduction**: Green witches actively participate in recycling programs and prioritize waste reduction. They practice responsible waste management by composting organic materials, reducing single-use plastics, and recycling items that can be repurposed or reused. They encourage others to adopt these practices and educate their communities about the importance of reducing waste.

1. **Conservation Efforts**: Green witches are advocates for environmental conservation. They may engage in activities such as supporting local conservation organizations, volunteering for habitat restoration projects, participating in tree planting initiatives, or advocating for the protection of natural areas and endangered species. They recognize the vital role of ecosystems and work to preserve biodiversity and maintain the balance of the natural world.

1. **Sustainable Gardening**: Green witches often cultivate their own gardens, practicing sustainable gardening methods. They prioritize organic gardening techniques, refrain from using harmful chemicals or pesticides, and focus on companion planting to promote natural pest control. They respect the cycles of the seasons, engage in water conservation practices, and prioritize the use of native plants that support local wildlife and pollinators.

1. **Ethical Foraging**: Green witches have a deep respect for the Earth's resources and practice ethical foraging. When gathering wild plants or herbs, they do so responsibly, ensuring that they are not depleting natural populations or damaging ecosystems. They take only what is needed, seeking permission from the plants, and leaving offerings of gratitude in return.

1. **Environmental Education**: Green witches are passionate about environmental education and raising awareness about ecological issues. They share their knowledge and experiences through workshops, classes, blogs, or social media platforms. They emphasize the interconnectedness of all living beings and the importance of individual and collective action in preserving the Earth's health.

1. **Rituals and Ceremonies for the Earth**: Green witches incorporate rituals and ceremonies dedicated to the Earth into their spiritual practice. These rituals may involve offerings, prayers, or energy work to honor and send healing energies to the Earth and its ecosystems. Green witches understand that these practices are not only spiritually significant but also serve as reminders of their responsibility as stewards of the environment.

1. **Advocacy and Activism**: Green witches are often active advocates for environmental causes. They may participate in rallies, marches, or campaigns to raise awareness about issues such as climate change, pollution, deforestation, or animal rights. They use their spiritual beliefs and practices as a foundation for their advocacy work, emphasizing the interconnectedness of all beings and the need for sustainable and compassionate action.

1. **Connection with Nature**: Green witches deepen their connection with nature through regular observation, contemplation, and spending time outdoors. They seek solace, inspiration, and guidance from the natural world, fostering a deep love and appreciation for the Earth. This connection fuels their commitment to environmental stewardship, as they recognize that protecting the Earth is vital for their own spiritual well-being and that of future generations.

Environmental stewardship is an integral part of the beliefs and practices of green witches. They actively engage in sustainable living, recycling, conservation efforts, sustainable gardening, ethical foraging, environmental education, rituals for the Earth, advocacy, and fostering a deep connection with nature. Through their actions and practices, green witches strive to be responsible caretakers of the Earth and inspire others to join in the collective effort of environmental stewardship.

Divination and Intuition

Divination and intuition are essential components of the spiritual practice of green witches. They rely on these tools to gain insight, guidance, and deeper understanding of themselves, their path, and the world around them. Green witches understand that divination and intuition are powerful means of accessing wisdom and knowledge beyond the physical realm. Here is an extensive description of divination and intuition with green witches:

1. **Divination Tools**: Green witches utilize various divination tools to access spiritual insights and guidance. Common tools include tarot cards, oracle cards, runes, pendulums, scrying mirrors, and divination bowls. Each tool has its own symbolism and method of interpretation. Green witches learn to connect with and interpret the messages received

through these tools, using them as a gateway to higher knowledge.

1. **Tarot Reading**: Tarot is a popular divination practice among green witches. They use tarot cards to explore the energies, archetypes, and symbolism represented in the deck. Green witches develop a deep relationship with their tarot decks, often choosing decks that resonate with their personal connection to nature. Through tarot readings, they gain insights into various aspects of their lives, including relationships, career, spiritual growth, and decision-making.

1. **Oracle Readings**: Green witches also work with oracle cards, which offer more flexibility and personalized interpretations compared to tarot. Oracle cards can have themes related to nature, animals, goddesses, elements, or other spiritual aspects. Green witches use oracle cards to connect with specific energies or receive guidance on particular areas of their lives. They trust their intuition to interpret the messages conveyed by the cards.

1. **Runes:** Runes are ancient symbols associated with the Germanic and Norse traditions. Green witches use rune stones or rune cards to tap into the wisdom of these symbols. Each rune represents a concept or energy, and by casting or drawing runes, green witches gain insights into various aspects of life. They interpret the patterns and combinations of runes intuitively, allowing the symbols to speak to them.

1. **Pendulum Work**: Green witches work with pendulums, which are typically a crystal, or a weighted object suspended on a chain or string. They use pendulums to receive yes or no answers, gain insights, or explore energetic imbalances. By asking questions and observing the movement

of the pendulum, green witches tap into their intuition to interpret the responses. Pendulum work helps them access their subconscious and receive guidance from higher realms.

1. **Scrying**: Scrying is a divination method that involves gazing into a reflective surface, such as a crystal ball, a black mirror, or a bowl of water. Green witches practice scrying to receive messages, visions, or symbols. They enter a meditative state and allow their intuitive senses to perceive information through the images or impressions that arise in the scrying medium. Scrying can be a deeply personal and introspective divination practice.

1. **Intuition and Inner Knowing**: Green witches place great emphasis on cultivating and trusting their intuition and inner knowing. They understand that intuition is a powerful tool for guidance and decision-making. Through regular meditation, mindfulness, and connection with nature, green witches deepen their intuitive abilities. They learn to listen to their inner voice, follow their instincts, and align with their highest purpose.

1. **Symbolism and Nature Signs**: Green witches pay close attention to symbolism and signs from nature as a form of divination. They observe patterns, synchronicities, and messages conveyed through animals, birds, plants, weather, or other natural elements. Green witches consider these encounters as messages from the divine or the universe, interpreting them as guidance or confirmation of their path.

1. **Dreamwork**: Green witches value the insights and guidance received through dreams. They keep dream journals, practice lucid dreaming, and engage in dream interpretation. They view dreams as a bridge

between the conscious and subconscious realms, where deep wisdom and messages can be revealed. Green witches pay attention to recurring symbols, emotions, or themes in their dreams, using them as sources of spiritual guidance.

1. **Meditation and Divination Rituals**: Green witches incorporate meditation and divination rituals into their practice to enhance their intuitive abilities. They create sacred space, connect with their breath, and enter a meditative state to quiet the mind and open themselves to receive guidance. They may combine divination tools, such as tarot cards or runes, with meditation to deepen their insights and interpretations.

Divination and intuition are integral to the spiritual practice of green witches. They utilize various divination tools, such as tarot cards, oracle cards, runes, pendulums, and scrying, to access spiritual insights and guidance. Green witches trust their intuition and inner knowing, recognizing them as powerful sources of wisdom. They also pay attention to symbolism, nature signs, dreams, and engage in meditation and divination rituals to further develop their intuitive abilities. Through divination and intuition, green witches seek clarity, guidance, and a deeper connection with the spiritual realms and the natural world.

Self-Sufficiency and Folklore

Self-sufficiency and folklore are important aspects of the green witch's lifestyle and spiritual practice. Green witches strive to be self-reliant, cultivating skills and knowledge that enable them to live in harmony with nature and create a sustainable and resilient life. They also draw inspiration from folklore, mythology, and traditional wisdom, integrating these rich cultural narratives into their practices. Here is an extensive description of self-sufficiency and folklore with green witches:

1. **Sustainable Living Skills**: Green witches prioritize self-sufficiency by acquiring practical skills that allow them to live more independently and in harmony with the Earth. They learn skills such as organic gardening, permaculture, food preservation, herbalism, natural building techniques, and renewable energy systems. These skills empower green witches to grow their own food, make their own natural remedies, reduce waste, and reduce their reliance on mainstream consumer culture.

1. **Homesteading and Traditional Crafts**: Green witches often embrace homesteading practices, seeking to create self-sufficient and sustainable homes. They may keep backyard chickens for eggs, learn traditional food preservation methods like canning and fermenting, and engage in woodworking, spinning, or weaving to create their own clothing or household items. By reviving these traditional skills, green witches connect with their ancestral heritage and build a closer relationship with the natural world.

1. **Herbal Folklore and Remedies**: Green witches draw inspiration from herbal folklore and traditional remedies passed down through generations. They study the medicinal properties of plants, including their historical uses, folklore, and associations with magical properties. Green witches gather and cultivate herbs, create herbal remedies, teas, and tinctures, and incorporate them into their healing practices. They honor the wisdom of herbal folklore, integrating it into their understanding of plant magic and holistic well-being.

1. **Folkloric Traditions and Celebrations**: Green witches celebrate and honor cultural folklore and traditions. They may observe seasonal festi-

vals, such as May Day or Midsummer, that have roots in ancient folklore and agricultural practices. Green witches participate in rituals, dances, or gatherings that connect them to the rhythms of the natural world and the wisdom of their ancestors. These celebrations serve as a way to honor and carry forward the rich cultural heritage associated with the cycles of nature.

1. **Mythology and Deity Worship**: Green witches draw inspiration from mythology and ancient pantheons, incorporating deities and spirits associated with nature into their practices. They may work with deities such as Artemis, Pan, Cernunnos, or Demeter, who embody natural forces and aspects of the Earth. Green witches engage in rituals, invocations, and offerings to honor and connect with these divine energies, seeking their guidance and blessings in their spiritual journey.

1. **Folk Magic and Spell work**: Green witches embrace the folk magic practices found in various cultural traditions. They may explore practices such as candle magic, charm-making, folk spells, or folk rituals passed down through generations. Green witches honor the wisdom embedded in these practices and adapt them to their own spiritual path, infusing them with their connection to nature and the Earth.

1. **Ancestral Connections**: Green witches recognize the importance of their ancestral lineage and seek to connect with the wisdom and traditions of their forebears. They explore their family history, traditions, and folk beliefs, integrating elements of their ancestral practices into their own spirituality. Green witches may incorporate ancestral altars, ancestral rituals, or ancestral divination to honor and commune with their lineage, drawing strength and guidance from the wisdom of their

ancestors.

1. **Storytelling and Oral Tradition**: Green witches appreciate the power of storytelling and the oral tradition. They share and pass on folklore, myths, and traditional tales through storytelling circles or written works. They understand the transformative and educational power of stories, which often contain valuable teachings, moral lessons, and insights into the relationship between humans and the natural world.

1. **Connection to the Land**: Green witches develop a deep connection to the land they inhabit. They study the local folklore, legends, and mythologies associated with the region. By honoring the land's history and cultural narratives, green witches form a deeper bond with the spirits of the land and the energies that flow through it. This connection fosters a sense of stewardship and responsibility for the local environment.

Green Witchcraft is a flexible and individualistic practice. While there may be shared themes and beliefs among Green Witches, each practitioner has their own unique approach and may incorporate other magical or spiritual traditions into their practice.

Green witches prioritize their connection to nature, the use of natural materials and resources, and the belief in the power of the Earth and its cycles. Their craft is centered around honoring and working with the energies and wisdom found in the natural world.

Chapter Thirty

Wiccan Protection Spell

It's important to note that spells should be performed with respect, intention, and ethical considerations.

PROTECTION SPELL

Create a protective amulet or charm using herbs, crystals, or symbols to ward off negative energies.

A Wiccan Protection Spell is a ritual designed to create a shield of spiritual protection around yourself, your space, or a loved one. It helps ward off negative energies, harmful influences, and psychic attacks. This spell aims to create a safe and protected environment for your well-being. Here are the instructions for a basic Wiccan Protection Spell:

Preparation: Choose a quiet and sacred space where you won't be disturbed.

Gather your materials, including a white candle, a small bowl of salt, a small bowl of water, and a protective crystal of your choice (such as black tourmaline or obsidian).

Clear your mind and ground yourself by taking a few deep breaths.

Casting the Circle: Start by visualizing a circle of light forming around you, expanding to create a sacred space. You can physically walk in a circle while visualizing or use your finger to trace the outline of the circle in the air.

Envision the circle as a barrier that keeps negative energies out and positive energies in.

Lighting the Candle: Light the white candle at the center of your sacred space, symbolizing purity and divine light. As you light the candle, say a simple invocation, such as: "I call upon the divine light to guide and protect me. May this flame be a beacon of safety and shield me from all harm."

Salt Purification: Take a pinch of salt from the bowl and hold it in your dominant hand. Close your eyes and visualize the salt glowing with protective energy.

Slowly sprinkle the salt around the perimeter of your sacred space, forming a protective boundary.

As you sprinkle the salt, recite: "By Earth's salt, I cast this protective ring. May it guard and shield me from all harm that may bring."

Water Cleansing: Take a moment to hold the bowl of water and feel its purifying energy.

Dip your fingertips into the water and lightly sprinkle it around your space, purifying the air.

Visualize the water cleansing the energy and removing any negative influences.

Say: "With Water's flow, I cleanse and purify. May this space be free from all negativity, both seen and unseen."

Crystal Protection: Hold the protective crystal in your hand and imbue it with your intention for protection.

Visualize a strong shield forming around you or the person you wish to protect, reflecting any negative energies back to their source.

Place the crystal near the candle or carry it with you as a talisman of protection.

Closing the Circle: Take a moment to express gratitude to the divine forces, elementals, or deities you may work with, for their protection and assistance.

Trace the outline of the circle in reverse, visualizing the energy being drawn back into yourself.

Extinguish the candle, knowing that the protection spell remains active.

Remember, this is a general protection spell, but you can personalize it by adding your own words, symbols, or additional elements that resonate with you. Always perform spells with positive intentions and respect for the free will of others.

Chapter Thirty-One

Wiccan Love Attraction Spell

A Wiccan Love Attraction Spell is designed to manifest love and draw a compatible romantic partner into your life. This spell focuses on enhancing your own magnetic energy and attracting love that aligns with your desires and intentions. It is important to approach this spell with pure intentions and an open heart. Here are the ingredients and instructions for a basic Wiccan Love Attraction Spell:

Ingredients:
Pink or red candle
Piece of paper
Pen or marker
Rose petals or dried herbs associated with love (e.g., rose, lavender)
Small pouch or cloth bag
Optional: love-drawing essential oil (e.g., rose, jasmine)

Preparation:
Choose a quiet and sacred space where you won't be disturbed.
Gather your materials and place them on your altar or clean surface.
Take a moment to ground yourself and set your intention for the spell.

Candle Preparation: Carve or write your name or initials on the candle, focusing on your desire for love and a compatible partner.

If desired, anoint the candle with a few drops of love-drawing essential oil, rubbing it from the base to the wick while visualizing love entering your life.

Setting Intentions: Take the piece of paper and write down the qualities and attributes you seek in a romantic partner. Be specific and focus on positive qualities that align with your values.

Visualize yourself already in a loving and fulfilling relationship as you write.

Fold the paper neatly, sealing your intentions within.

Candle Ritual: Light the pink or red candle, symbolizing love and passion.

Hold the folded paper in your hands and infuse it with your intentions and desires.

Gently pass the paper through the flame of the candle, visualizing the flame igniting the energy of love and attraction.

Place the paper in a fire-safe container to let it burn completely or keep it safe until the end of the spell.

Affirmations and Visualization: Close your eyes and visualize yourself surrounded by a warm, loving energy.

Repeat affirmations that reinforce your intention, such as: "I am open to love. I attract a loving and compatible partner into my life. Love flows to me effortlessly."

See yourself engaging in activities with your ideal partner, feeling the love and happiness you desire.

Love Talisman: Take the rose petals or dried herbs and place them inside the small pouch or cloth bag.

Hold the pouch in your hands and infuse it with the energy of love and attraction.

Visualize the pouch radiating a vibrant energy that draws love towards you.

Carry the pouch with you or place it in a safe and sacred place, such as your bedside table or under your pillow, to continue attracting love.

Gratitude and Closure: Express gratitude to the universe, deities, or forces you work with, thanking them for their assistance in manifesting love.

Blow out the candle, knowing that the spell has been set in motion.

Take a few moments to ground yourself and release any attachment to the outcome, trusting that love will come to you in divine timing.

Remember that this spell is intended to enhance your own magnetic energy and attract love into your life. It is essential to maintain an open heart, be patient, and remain receptive to the opportunities and connections that come your way.

Chapter Thirty-Two

Wiccan Healing Spell

A Wiccan Healing Spell is a ritual designed to promote physical, emotional, or spiritual healing. This spell aims to channel healing energy and support the restoration of balance and well-being. It can be performed for yourself, a loved one, or even for sending healing energy to a specific situation or area. Here are the ingredients and instructions for a basic Wiccan Healing Spell:

Ingredients:

Blue or green candle (representing healing and harmony)
Healing crystals or stones (such as clear quartz, amethyst, or rose quartz)
Healing herbs or essential oils (such as lavender, eucalyptus, or chamomile)
Small bowl of water
Piece of paper
Pen or marker

Preparation:

Choose a quiet and sacred space where you won't be disturbed.

Gather your materials and place them on your altar or clean surface.

Take a few moments to center yourself, clear your mind, and set your intention for the spell.

Candle Preparation:

Light the blue or green candle, representing healing energy.

Hold the candle in your hands and visualize it being infused with healing energy.

State your intention for healing, either silently or aloud, such as: "I call upon the healing powers of the universe to flow through this candle and bring forth healing and harmony."

Crystal and Herb Placement:

Arrange the healing crystals or stones around the candle, forming a circle or any pattern that feels intuitive to you.

Place the healing herbs or a few drops of essential oil near the crystals, allowing their scent to fill the space with healing energy.

Water Blessing:

Hold the small bowl of water in your hands, visualizing it being filled with healing energy.

You can add a few drops of healing essential oil or sprinkle some healing herbs into the water for additional potency.

State your intention for healing as you hold the water, such as: "I bless this water with healing energy, and as it touches those in need, may it bring comfort, restoration, and well-being."

Healing Affirmations:

Take the piece of paper and write down the name of the person or situation that requires healing.

Visualize the person or situation surrounded by a warm, healing light.

Repeat healing affirmations, either silently or aloud, focusing on positive outcomes and well-being.

Fold the paper neatly and place it in the vicinity of the candles, crystals, and herbs.

Channeling Healing Energy:

Close your eyes and visualize healing energy flowing from the candle, crystals, and herbs towards the person or situation in need.

Visualize the energy enveloping and penetrating the person or situation, bringing comfort, balance, and restoration.

Hold this image in your mind for as long as it feels appropriate, sending healing energy with love and compassion.

Gratitude and Closure: Express gratitude to the universe, deities, or forces you work with, thanking them for their assistance in facilitating healing.

Blow out the candle, knowing that the spell has been set in motion and the healing energy will continue its work.

Take a few moments to ground yourself, release any attachment to the outcome, and trust in the healing process.

Remember, this spell is intended to support the healing process and promote well-being. It is not a substitute for professional medical or mental health assistance. Always seek appropriate medical care and consult with a healthcare professional for any health concerns.

Chapter Thirty-Three

Wiccan Prosperity Spell

A Wiccan Prosperity Spell is a ritual designed to attract abundance, wealth, and prosperity into your life. This spell focuses on aligning your energy with the vibrations of prosperity and creating a mindset of abundance. It is important to approach this spell with gratitude and a positive outlook. Here are the ingredients and instructions for a basic Wiccan Prosperity Spell:

Ingredients

Green candle (representing abundance and prosperity)

A small dish or bowl

Bay leaves or cinnamon sticks

A small pouch or cloth bag

Optional: Money-drawing herbs or essential oils (such as basil, mint, or patchouli)

Preparation:

Choose a quiet and sacred space where you won't be disturbed.

Gather your materials and place them on your altar or clean surface.

Take a moment to ground yourself and set your intention for the spell.

Candle Preparation:

Light the green candle, symbolizing abundance and prosperity.

Hold the candle in your hands and visualize it being infused with the energy of prosperity and financial well-being.

State your intention for prosperity, either silently or aloud, such as: "I call upon the energies of abundance and prosperity to flow through this candle and manifest in my life."

Prosperity Symbols:

Write down your desired financial goals or affirmations on the bay leaves or cinnamon sticks.

Visualize these goals as already achieved, feeling the excitement and gratitude associated with them.

Place the bay leaves or cinnamon sticks in the small dish or bowl, creating a collection of your intentions.

Charging the Symbols:

Hold your hands over the bay leaves or cinnamon sticks and visualize them being charged with vibrant energy.

You can also sprinkle a few drops of money-drawing essential oil or rub the herbs between your fingers to further enhance their energy.

Abundance Visualization:

Close your eyes and imagine yourself surrounded by a golden light of abundance.

Visualize money and opportunities flowing effortlessly into your life, bringing financial prosperity and security.

Feel the emotions of gratitude and abundance as you immerse yourself in this visualization.

Placing the Symbols:

Take the charged bay leaves or cinnamon sticks and place them in the small pouch or cloth bag.

Hold the pouch in your hands, infusing it with the energy of prosperity and abundance.

Visualize the pouch radiating a vibrant energy that attracts wealth and prosperity.

Carry the pouch with you or place it in a safe and sacred place, such as your purse or a drawer in your home, as a reminder of your intentions.

Gratitude and Closure:

Express gratitude to the universe, deities, or forces you work with, thanking them for their assistance in manifesting prosperity.

Blow out the candle, knowing that the spell has been set in motion and the energy of abundance is working in your favor.

Take a few moments to ground yourself and release any attachment to the outcome, trusting that opportunities for prosperity will come to you.

Remember that this spell is intended to align your energy with prosperity and open doors for abundance. It is important to take inspired action and make practical choices in your pursuit of prosperity. The spell serves as a catalyst and reinforcement of your intentions, but it is up to you to actively seek and seize opportunities.

Chapter Thirty-Four

Wiccan Cleansing Spell

A Wiccan Cleansing Spell is a ritual designed to purify and cleanse your energy, your living space, or any objects you wish to clear of negative or stagnant energy. This spell helps to restore balance, harmony, and a sense of renewal. It is important to approach this spell with intention and focus on releasing what no longer serves you. Here are the ingredients and instructions for a basic Wiccan Cleansing Spell:

Ingredients:
White candle (representing purity and cleansing)
Bowl of water
Salt or sea salt
Incense or smudging tool (such as sage, cedar, or palo santo)
Optional: Cleansing herbs or essential oils (such as lavender, rosemary, or lemon)

Preparation:

Choose a quiet and sacred space where you won't be disturbed.

Gather your materials and place them on your altar or clean surface.

Take a moment to ground yourself and set your intention for the spell.

Candle Preparation:

Light the white candle, symbolizing purity and cleansing.

Hold the candle in your hands and visualize it being filled with a bright, purifying light.

State your intention for cleansing, either silently or aloud, such as: "I call upon the energies of purity and renewal to flow through this candle and cleanse all that is in need of release."

Water Blessing:

Hold the bowl of water in your hands and visualize it being infused with cleansing energy.

Add a pinch of salt or sea salt to the water, symbolizing purification and the removal of negative energy.

You can also add a few drops of cleansing herbs or essential oils to enhance the energy of the water.

State your intention for cleansing as you hold the water, such as: "I bless this water with cleansing energy, and as it touches, may it wash away all negativity and restore harmony and balance."

Incense or Smudging:

Light the incense or smudging tool, allowing the smoke to fill the space.

Begin at the entrance of your living space or the area you wish to cleanse and move clockwise, gently waving the smoke with a feather or your hand.

Visualize the smoke purifying and dispelling any stagnant or negative energy, leaving behind a sense of renewal and harmony.

Focus on areas or objects that you feel require extra cleansing or have accumulated negative energy.

Personal Cleansing:

Stand or sit comfortably and close your eyes.

Visualize a beam of pure, white light descending from above and surrounding your body.

Imagine this light purifying and cleansing your energy, releasing any negativity, tension, or stagnant emotions.

Take deep breaths, inhaling positivity and exhaling negativity, allowing yourself to feel lighter and refreshed.

Gratitude and Closure:

Express gratitude to the universe, deities, or forces you work with, thanking them for their assistance in the cleansing process.

Blow out the candle, knowing that the spell has been set in motion and the energy of purification is working.

Take a few moments to ground yourself, release any remaining tension or negativity, and embrace the sense of renewal and harmony.

Remember, this spell serves as a tool to support your own intention and efforts in cleansing and purifying. It is important to regularly practice self-care and maintain a positive and balanced energy in your living space. Feel free to adapt and personalize this spell to align with your own beliefs and practices.

Chapter Thirty-Five

Wiccan Protection Jar Spell

A Wiccan Protection Jar Spell is a ritual that utilizes the power of intention, herbs, crystals, and other protective elements to create a physical representation of protection and ward off negative energies. This spell is designed to create a shield of protection around you or your living space. The jar serves as a container to hold the protective energies and keep them working continuously. Here are the ingredients and instructions for a basic Wiccan Protection Jar Spell:

Ingredients:
Glass jar with a tight-fitting lid
Protective herbs (such as rosemary, sage, basil, or bay leaves)
Protective crystals or stones (such as black tourmaline, amethyst, or hematite)
Sea salt or black salt
Protective symbols (such as a pentagram, runes, or sigils)
Paper and pen
Optional: Personal items or talismans for additional connection and protection

Preparation:

Choose a quiet and sacred space where you won't be disturbed.

Gather your materials and place them on your altar or clean surface.

Take a moment to ground yourself and set your intention for the spell.

Cleansing the Jar:

Start by cleansing the glass jar to remove any residual energy. You can do this by washing it with soap and water or smudging it with incense or sage.

Protective Herb Placement:

Place a layer of the protective herbs at the bottom of the jar. You can use a single herb or a mixture of herbs that resonate with protection and warding off negativity.

As you place each herb, focus your intention on their protective properties and their ability to create a shield of protection around you or your space.

Charging the Crystals:

Hold each protective crystal or stone in your hands, one at a time.

Visualize the crystal being filled with vibrant protective energy and imagine a shield forming around it.

State your intention for protection, either silently or aloud, such as: "I charge this crystal with the power of protection. May it radiate its energy to shield and safeguard me from all negativity."

Crystal Placement:

Add the charged crystals or stones on top of the layer of herbs inside the jar.

Arrange them in a way that feels harmonious and balanced to you, imagining their protective energy amplifying and intertwining.

Protective Symbol and Personal Items:

Write down protective symbols, sigils, or runes on a small piece of paper.

You can also add personal items, such as a small piece of jewelry or a token that holds meaning for you and represents protection.

Place the paper with the symbols and any personal items inside the jar, on top of the herbs and crystals.

Salt Layer:

Add a layer of sea salt or black salt to the jar, covering the herbs, crystals, symbols, and personal items.

Salt has long been associated with protection and cleansing, creating a barrier against negativity.

Sealing and Activating the Jar:

Close the jar tightly, ensuring that it is securely sealed.

Hold the jar in your hands and visualize a powerful shield forming around it, extending its protective energy outward.

State your intention for protection, either silently or aloud, such as: "I activate this jar as a powerful protector. May it ward off negativity and create a safe and sacred space."

Placement and Maintenance

Find a suitable place for the protection jar where it won't be disturbed.

You can keep it on your altar, a shelf, or in a hidden spot in your living space.

Periodically, you can recharge the energy of the jar by holding it in your hands, visualizing its protective energy being renewed, and stating your intention for continued protection.

Remember, the power of the protection jar comes from your intention and the energy you infuse into it. You can personalize this spell by using herbs, crystals, symbols, or items that resonate with your own beliefs and practices. Trust your intuition and make adjustments as needed to align with your unique path.

Chapter Thirty-Six

Wiccan Banishing Spell

A Wiccan Banishing Spell is a ritual designed to release and remove negative energies, influences, or situations from your life. This spell empowers you to let go of what no longer serves you and create space for positive energies and new beginnings. It is important to approach this spell with clarity, focus, and a strong intention for release. Here are the ingredients and instructions for a basic Wiccan Banishing Spell:

Ingredients:
Black candle (representing the removal of negativity)
Athame or a sharp object (such as a needle or pin)
Paper and pen
Optional: Banishing herbs or essential oils (such as rosemary, sage, or frankincense)
Optional: A fire-safe container or cauldron

Preparation:

Choose a quiet and sacred space where you won't be disturbed.

Gather your materials and place them on your altar or clean surface.

Take a moment to ground yourself and set your intention for the spell.

Candle Preparation:

Light the black candle, symbolizing the removal of negativity and unwanted influences.

Hold the candle in your hands and visualize it being infused with the energy of banishment.

State your intention for banishing, either silently or aloud, such as: "I call upon the energies of removal and release to flow through this candle and assist in the banishment of all that no longer serves me."

Identification of Negative Energies:

Take the paper and pen and write down the negative energies, situations, or influences that you wish to banish from your life.

Be specific and concise in your descriptions, focusing on what you want to release.

Visualize these negative energies being transferred from your mind onto the paper, effectively externalizing them.

Release Ritual:

Hold the paper in your hands and focus on the negative energies described on it.

With a strong intention for release, use the athame or sharp object to pierce through the paper, symbolizing the breaking of ties with these energies.

As you pierce the paper, visualize the negative energies being severed and dissipated, leaving your life completely.

Affirmation of Release:

Hold the pierced paper over the flame of the black candle.

As it catches fire, repeat an affirmation of release, such as: "I release and banish all negative energies. I am free from their influence. As this paper burns, I am cleansed and renewed."

Burning of the Paper:

Safely place the burning paper in a fire-safe container or cauldron, allowing it to burn completely.

Visualize the flames transforming the negative energies into ash, symbolizing their permanent removal from your life.

As the paper burns, feel a sense of liberation and relief.

Cleansing and Grounding:

After the paper has burned, extinguish the black candle.

Take a few deep breaths, inhaling positivity and exhaling any residual negativity.

You can perform a personal cleansing ritual, such as taking a ritual bath or smudging yourself with purifying herbs.

Gratitude and Closure:

Express gratitude to the universe, deities, or forces you work with, thanking them for their assistance in the banishing process.

Take a moment to reflect on the sense of release and freedom that comes with letting go of what no longer serves you.

Ground yourself and close the ritual, knowing that you have created space for positive energies and new beginnings.

Remember, this spell is a powerful tool to support your intention for banishing negative energies. It is important to take responsibility for your own actions and decisions and actively seek positive

Chapter Thirty-Seven

Wiccan Moon Magic Spell

Moon magic is an integral part of Wiccan practices, as the cycles of the moon are believed to influence our energy and intentions. Performing a Wiccan Moon Magic Spell allows you to harness the specific energies of each lunar phase and work with them to manifest your desires. This spell can be tailored to the specific lunar phase you wish to work with, such as the New Moon for new beginnings or the Full Moon for amplifying intentions. Here are the ingredients and instructions for a basic Wiccan Moon Magic Spell:

Ingredients:
Candle (color corresponding to the specific lunar phase)
Altar or sacred space
Crystals or gemstones (optional, chosen based on your intention)
Journal or paper and pen
Optional: Herbs, essential oils, or incense (chosen based on your intention)

Preparation:

Choose a quiet and sacred space where you won't be disturbed.

Set up your altar or clean surface with your materials.

Take a moment to ground yourself and align with the energy of the moon phase you wish to work with.

Setting Your Intention:

Take your journal or paper and pen and write down your intention for this Moon Magic Spell.

Be clear and concise in your intention, focusing on what you wish to manifest or release.

Visualize your intention as if it has already come to fruition, feeling the emotions and sensations associated with it.

Candle Selection:

Choose a candle that corresponds to the specific lunar phase you are working with. For example:

New Moon: Black or dark blue candle for new beginnings and setting intentions.

Waxing Moon: Light blue or silver candle for growth, manifestation, and attracting desires.

Full Moon: White or yellow candle for amplifying intentions and working with the moon's powerful energy.

Waning Moon: Dark or purple candle for releasing, banishing, and letting go.

Cleansing and Charging:

If desired, cleanse and charge your crystals or gemstones by holding them in your hands and visualizing them being filled with the energy of the moon phase you are working with.

You can also cleanse and charge any herbs, essential oils, or incense by passing them through the smoke of the candle or smudging them with sacred herbs.

Ritual:

Light the candle, symbolizing the energy and power of the moon phase.

Take a few moments to gaze at the flame, connecting with its energy and the energy of your intention.

Hold your crystals or gemstones (if using) in your hands and visualize your intention merging with their energy.

Affirmation and Visualization:

Speak your intention aloud or silently, affirming it with confidence and belief.

Visualize your intention manifesting under the influence of the moon phase, seeing it clearly and vividly in your mind.

Optional Additional Steps:

If desired, you can anoint the candle with a small amount of essential oil or sprinkle herbs associated with your intention around the candle.

You may also choose to perform a guided meditation, chant a mantra, or incorporate other rituals that resonate with you.

Closing the Ritual:

Express gratitude to the moon and the energy of the lunar phase you worked with.

Blow out the candle, releasing the energy into the universe.

Keep your journal or paper with your intention somewhere safe and refer to it throughout the lunar cycle.

Remember, moon magic is a personal practice, and you can adapt and customize this spell to align with your own beliefs and practices. Trust your intuition and work with the moon's energy in a way that feels most authentic

Chapter Thirty-Eight

Wiccan Divination Spell

A Wiccan Divination Spell is a ritual that enables practitioners to gain insight and guidance through divinatory tools such as tarot cards, runes, or scrying. This spell is performed to connect with higher spiritual energies and receive messages and wisdom from the universe. It allows you to tap into your intuition and receive answers to questions or seek guidance on specific areas of your life. Here are the ingredients and instructions for a Wiccan Divination Spell:

Ingredients:

Divinatory tool of your choice (tarot cards, runes, scrying mirror, pendulum, etc.)

Candle (color can be chosen based on your intention or the element associated with your divinatory tool)

Altar or sacred space

Optional: Incense or herbs for enhancing psychic abilities and focus

Optional: Journal or paper and pen to record your readings and interpretations

Preparation:

Choose a quiet and sacred space where you won't be disturbed.

Set up your altar or clean surface with your divinatory tool and candle.

If desired, light incense or place herbs associated with psychic abilities nearby to create a focused and conducive atmosphere.

Grounding and Centering:

Take a few moments to ground yourself and center your energy.

Close your eyes and take deep, calming breaths, allowing any distractions or tensions to fade away.

Visualize yourself becoming grounded, rooted, and connected to the Earth's energy.

Cleansing and Charging:

If you are using a divinatory tool such as tarot cards or runes, take a moment to cleanse and charge them.

You can pass them through the smoke of the candle or use other cleansing methods such as visualization or sound.

Setting Your Intention:

Light the candle, symbolizing the illumination of wisdom and spiritual insight.

State your intention aloud or silently, expressing your desire to receive guidance and insights from the divinatory tool.

Focus on your intention and visualize a connection being established between yourself and the higher spiritual energies.

Connecting with the Divinatory Tool:

Hold your divinatory tool in your hands, feeling its energy and connection with your own.

Take a moment to connect with the tool, establishing a psychic link and attuning yourself to its vibrations.

If you are using tarot cards, shuffle them while focusing on your question or the area of your life you seek guidance on.

Asking Your Question:

State your question or intention clearly in your mind or aloud, directing it towards the divinatory tool.

Focus your attention on the question, allowing it to resonate within you.

Performing the Divination:

Use your divinatory tool to conduct the reading according to its specific method or system.

Trust your intuition and interpret the messages and symbols you receive.

Take your time with the reading, allowing the insights to unfold and guide you.

Recording and Reflecting:

If you have a journal or paper and pen, write down the results of your divination, including any specific symbols or impressions that stood out to you.

Reflect on the messages and insights you received, considering how they apply to your situation or question.

Use this information to inform your decisions, actions, or further exploration.

Closing the Ritual:

Thank the divinatory tool, the universe, or any deities or spirits you work with for their guidance and presence.

Extinguish the candle, symbolizing the completion of the divination ritual.

Store your divinatory tool safely, ensuring it remains cleansed and protected until its next use.

Remember, divination is a practice that requires focus, openness, and trust in your intuition. Each divination tool may have its own specific instructions and interpretations, so it is essential to familiarize yourself with its usage. As you gain experience and confidence, you can adapt and personalize the ritual to suit your unique style of divination

Chapter Thirty-Nine

Wiccan Binding Spell

A Wiccan Binding Spell is a ritual that is performed to create energetic boundaries, protect oneself or others, and prevent harm. It can be used to bind negative energies, harmful influences, or even to bind oneself from engaging in negative behaviors. This spell is intended to promote safety, harmony, and personal empowerment.

Ingredients:

Black cord, string, or ribbon (length depends on your preference)
Small piece of paper or parchment
Pen or marker
Altar or sacred space
Optional: Protective herbs, such as sage or rosemary
Optional: Protective crystals, such as black tourmaline or obsidian

Preparation:

Choose a quiet and sacred space where you won't be disturbed.

Set up your altar or clean surface with your materials.

Take a moment to ground yourself and center your energy.

Setting Your Intention:

Take the small piece of paper or parchment and write down your intention for the binding spell.

Be clear and specific about what you want to bind or protect yourself or others from.

Visualize your intention as if it has already been achieved, feeling the sense of safety and empowerment it brings.

Cord Preparation:

Hold the black cord, string, or ribbon in your hands.

Focus on its purpose as a symbol of binding and protection.

If desired, you can infuse the cord with protective energy by passing it through the smoke of protective herbs or overprotective crystals.

Binding Ritual:

With the cord in your hands, recite your intention aloud or silently, infusing it with your focused energy.

Visualize the cord binding and wrapping around the negative energies or influences, preventing them from causing harm.

As you visualize this, physically wrap the cord around the piece of paper or parchment, symbolizing the binding.

Sealing the Binding:

Tie a knot at the end of the cord, securing the binding.

As you tie the knot, affirm your intention and state that the binding is in effect.

You may choose to tie additional knots, each representing a layer of protection and strengthening the binding.

Charging the Binding:

Hold the bound cord in your hands, feeling its energy and power.

Speak words of empowerment and protection, such as: "By the power of my intention, this binding is strong and secure, protecting me and all involved."

Placement:

Decide where to place the bound cord. You may choose to keep it on your altar, bury it in the ground, or hide it in a safe place.

Closing the Ritual:

Express gratitude to the energies or deities you called upon for their assistance and protection.

Close the ritual by extinguishing any candles or clearing the space as desired.

A binding spell should be performed with a clear and responsible intention. It is important to respect the free will of others and use this spell for protection and harm prevention rather than manipulation. Use your own ethical judgment and only direct this spell towards situations or individuals where it is truly necessary for the greater good.

Chapter Forty

Wiccan Self-Confidence spell

The Wiccan Self-Confidence spell is a ritual designed to help individuals enhance their self-esteem and develop a positive sense of self-worth. It aims to empower individuals and cultivate a deep belief in their abilities and worthiness. Here is a full description of the Wiccan self-confidence spell:

Ingredients:
- White candle
- Small mirror
- Piece of paper
- Pen or marker
- Essential oil (optional)
- Incense (optional)
- Clear quartz crystal (optional)

Preparation:

Find a quiet and comfortable space where you can perform the spell without interruptions.

Cleanse and purify the space by burning incense or using any method that resonates with you.

Gather all the ingredients and place them within reach.

Setting Intentions:

Take a few deep breaths to ground yourself and focus your mind.

Light the white candle, symbolizing purity and clarity of intention.

Hold the mirror in your hands and visualize radiant confidence and self-assuredness filling your being.

State your intention clearly, such as "I am worthy, confident, and deserving of all the good things in my life."

Writing Affirmations

Take the piece of paper and write down positive affirmations about yourself and your abilities.

Choose statements that resonate with you and reflect the qualities you want to embody.

Examples could be: "I am confident and capable," "I embrace my uniqueness and shine my light," or "I am worthy of love and success."

Write them in the present tense, as if they are already true.

Empowering the Affirmations

Read each affirmation aloud, allowing the words to resonate within you.

Envision yourself embodying each affirmation, feeling the confidence and self-assurance growing within you.

As you read each affirmation, visualize the words being absorbed into the mirror, infusing it with positive energy.

Charging the Mirror

If desired, anoint the mirror with a few drops of essential oil that enhances confidence, such as rosemary or bergamot.

Hold the mirror up to the candle flame, allowing the light to reflect onto the mirror's surface.
Visualize the mirror absorbing the empowering energy from the flame, becoming a powerful tool for self-reflection and confidence.

Affirmation Activation:

Hold the mirror in front of you and investigate your own reflection.

Repeat each affirmation aloud, gazing into your own eyes and allowing the words to sink deeply into your subconscious.

Feel the energy of confidence and self-assurance radiating from the mirror and into your being.

Closing the Ritual

Express gratitude to the Universe, the Divine, or any deities or spirits you work with for their guidance and support.

Snuff out the candle, acknowledging the end of the ritual and the beginning of your empowered journey.

Keep the mirror and the affirmations in a safe place, using them as reminders of your self-confidence whenever needed.

The power of any spell lies within your intentions and belief. The Wiccan self-confidence spell is a tool to help you tap into your inner strength and cultivate a positive mindset. Embrace the process with an open heart and mind, and trust in your own abilities to manifest self-confidence and empowerment.

Chapter Forty-One

Wiccan Communication Spell

A Wiccan Communication Spell is a ritual designed to enhance and improve communication between individuals. This spell can be used to promote understanding, clarity, and effective communication in various relationships, such as romantic partnerships, friendships, or even professional connections. It aims to open channels of communication, encourage honest expression, and foster harmony in relationships. Here are the ingredients and instructions for a basic Wiccan Communication Spell:

Ingredients:

Blue candle (representing clear communication)
Piece of paper or parchment
Pen or marker
Altar or sacred space
Optional: Communication-enhancing herbs, such as lavender or chamomile
Optional: Communication-enhancing crystals, such as blue lace agate or sodalite

Preparation:

Choose a quiet and sacred space where you won't be disturbed.

Set up your altar or clean surface with your materials.

Take a moment to ground yourself and center your energy.

Setting Your Intention:

Take the piece of paper or parchment and write down your intention for the communication spell.

Be clear and specific about what you want to improve or achieve in your communication.

Visualize yourself and the other person engaged in open, honest, and understanding dialogue.

Candle Preparation:

Light the blue candle, symbolizing clear and effective communication.

Hold the candle in your hands and infuse it with the energy of open and harmonious communication.

State your intention for the spell, either silently or aloud, such as: "I call upon the energies of clear communication and understanding to improve and strengthen the connection between myself and [person's name]."

Written Affirmation:

On the piece of paper or parchment, write down affirmations or positive statements regarding the desired communication outcome.

For example: "Our words flow with ease and understanding," "We listen to each other with empathy and respect," or "Our communication brings us closer together."

Charging the Affirmation:

Hold the written affirmation in your hands and visualize the energy of clear communication infusing the words on the paper.

Read the affirmations aloud, putting your intention and energy into each statement.

Optional Herbal or Crystal Use:

If you have chosen to work with communication-enhancing herbs or crystals, hold them in your hands and visualize their energy merging with your own.

Feel their supportive and calming vibrations enhancing your communication abilities.

Affirmation Burning:

Hold the written affirmation over the flame of the blue candle, allowing it to catch fire.

As it burns, visualize the energy of the words being released into the universe, carrying your intentions for improved communication.

Closing the Ritual:

Express gratitude to yourself, the universe, or any deities or spirits you work with, acknowledging the growth and connection that comes from clear communication.

Blow out the candle, releasing the energy into the universe.

Take a moment to reflect on the work you have done and the positive energy you have invoked.

Effective communication also requires active listening, empathy, and understanding. This spell is a tool to support and enhance your communication skills, but it is important to practice these skills in your daily interactions as well. Be patient, open-minded, and compassionate as you strive for improved communication in your relationships.

Chapter Forty-Two

Wiccan Friendship Spell

A Wiccan Friendship Spell is a ritual designed to attract new friendships or strengthen existing ones. This spell is intended to create a positive and harmonious energy that draws like-minded individuals into your life, fostering deep and meaningful connections. It can also be used to heal and mend broken friendships. The goal of this spell is to promote friendship, companionship, and mutual support. Here are the ingredients and instructions for a basic Wiccan Friendship Spell:

Ingredients:
Pink candle (representing love and friendship)
Small piece of paper or parchment
Pen or marker
Altar or sacred space
Optional: Friendship-enhancing herbs, such as lavender or rose petals
Optional: Friendship-enhancing crystals, such as rose quartz or green aventurine

Preparation

Choose a quiet and sacred space where you won't be disturbed.

Set up your altar or clean surface with your materials.

Take a moment to ground yourself and center your energy.

Setting Your Intention:

Take the small piece of paper or parchment and write down your intention for the friendship spell.

Be clear and specific about the qualities you seek in friendships or the particular friendship you wish to strengthen.

Visualize yourself surrounded by genuine friends who share your interests, values, and support you.

Candle Preparation:

Light the pink candle, symbolizing love and friendship.

Hold the candle in your hands and infuse it with the energy of friendship, love, and companionship.

State your intention for the spell, either silently or aloud, such as: "I open myself to attracting genuine friendships that bring joy, support, and love into my life."

Written Affirmation:

On the piece of paper or parchment, write down affirmations or positive statements about the qualities you seek in friendships or the friendship you want to strengthen.

For example: "I attract friends who are loyal and supportive," "My friendships are based on trust and understanding," or "My friendship with [friend's name] is strong and filled with love."

Charging the Affirmation:

Hold the written affirmation in your hands and visualize the energy of friendship and love infusing the words on the paper.

Read the affirmations aloud, putting your intention and energy into each statement.

Optional Herbal or Crystal Use:

If you have chosen to work with friendship-enhancing herbs or crystals, hold them in your hands and visualize their energy merging with your own.

Feel their supportive and loving vibrations attracting and nurturing positive friendships.

Affirmation Burning:

Hold the written affirmation over the flame of the pink candle, allowing it to catch fire.

As it burns, visualize the energy of your intentions being released into the universe, attracting and nurturing loving friendships.

Closing the Ritual:

Express gratitude to yourself, the universe, or any deities or spirits you work with, acknowledging the friendships you have and the ones that are yet to come.

Blow out the candle, releasing the energy into the universe.

Take a moment to reflect on the positive energy you have invoked and the openness you have created for new friendships.

Friendship is a two-way street, and building and maintaining meaningful connections requires effort and genuine care. This spell is a tool to attract and nurture friendships, but it is important to actively engage in social activities, be open to new experiences, and be a good friend yourself. Practice kindness, empathy, and authenticity to create and sustain deep and fulfilling friendships.

Chapter Forty-Three

Wiccan Moon Magic Spell

A Wiccan Moon Magic Spell is a ritual performed to invite the energies of fertility, whether it's physical fertility for conceiving a child or symbolic fertility for new beginnings and creative projects. This spell aims to connect with the cycles of nature, the divine feminine, and the energy of creation. It encourages the flow of life and abundance. Here are the ingredients and instructions for a basic Wiccan Fertility Spell:

Ingredients:
Red or green candle (representing fertility, passion, and growth)
Small bowl of soil or earth
Piece of paper or parchment
Pen or marker
Altar or sacred space
Optional: Fertility-enhancing herbs such as nettle, red raspberry leaf, or chamomile
Optional: Fertility-enhancing crystals such as moonstone, carnelian, or rose quartz

Preparation:

Find a quiet and sacred space where you can perform the spell without distractions.

Set up your altar or clean surface with your materials.

Take a few deep breaths to center yourself and connect with the energy of the earth.

Setting Your Intention:

Take the piece of paper or parchment and write down your intention for the fertility spell.

Be clear and specific about what you desire to manifest, whether it's physical fertility, new opportunities, or creative projects.

Visualize your intention coming to fruition, feeling the joy and abundance it brings.

Candle Preparation:

Light the red or green candle, symbolizing fertility, passion, and growth.

Hold the candle in your hands, infusing it with your intention and the energy of fertility.

State your intention for the spell, either silently or aloud, such as: "I embrace the fertile energy of the earth and invite the flow of abundance and creation into my life."

Connection to the Earth:

Take the small bowl of soil or earth and hold it in your hands.

Feel a deep connection with the earth's nurturing energy and the potential for growth and life.

If using a bowl of soil, you can also envision it as a symbol of fertile ground ready to receive your intentions.

Written Affirmation:

On the piece of paper or parchment, write down affirmations or positive statements related to fertility or your desired outcome.

For example: "My body is fertile and ready to conceive," "I attract new opportunities and abundance," or "My creative projects flourish and bring joy."

Charging the Affirmation:

Hold the written affirmation in your hands and visualize the energy of fertility and abundance infusing the words on the paper.

Read the affirmations aloud, putting your intention and energy into each statement.

Optional Herbal or Crystal Use:

If you have chosen to work with fertility-enhancing herbs or crystals, hold them in your hands and visualize their energy merging with your own.

Feel their nurturing and fertile vibrations supporting your intentions.

Affirmation Planting:

Bury the written affirmation in the soil or sprinkle it over the earth in your bowl.

As you do this, visualize your intentions being planted in fertile ground, ready to sprout and grow.

Closing the Ritual:

Express gratitude to yourself, the earth, or any deities or spirits you work with, acknowledging the fertility and abundance in your life.

Blow out the candle, releasing the energy into the universe.

Take a moment to reflect on the energy you have invoked and the potential for growth and creation.

Remember, fertility spells are personal and should align with your own beliefs and desires. Trust in the power of your intention, and be open to receiving the blessings of fertility and abundance in all their forms.

Chapter Forty-Four

Wiccan Intuition Spell

A Wiccan Intuition Spell is a ritual performed to enhance your intuitive abilities and connect with your inner wisdom. This spell aims to open and strengthen your intuitive channels, allowing you to trust your instincts, receive guidance, and make decisions with clarity. It encourages a deeper connection with the divine and the unseen realms.

Ingredients:

Purple or indigo candle (representing intuition, spiritual insight, and higher consciousness)
Small bowl of water
Piece of amethyst or clear quartz crystal
Piece of paper or parchment
Pen or marker
Altar or sacred space
Optional: Intuition-enhancing herbs such as mugwort or lavender
Optional: Divination tools such as tarot cards or a pendulum

Preparation:

Find a quiet and sacred space where you can perform the spell without distractions.

Set up your altar or clean surface with your materials.

Take a moment to center yourself and enter a relaxed state of mind.

Setting Your Intention:

Take the piece of paper or parchment and write down your intention for the intuition spell.

Be clear and specific about what you desire to enhance or receive guidance in.

Visualize yourself tapping into your intuitive abilities, trusting your inner voice, and accessing higher wisdom.

Candle Preparation:

Light the purple or indigo candle, symbolizing intuition, spiritual insight, and higher consciousness.

Hold the candle in your hands, infusing it with your intention and the energy of intuition.

State your intention for the spell, either silently or aloud, such as: "I embrace and honor my intuition, connecting with the divine wisdom within me."

Connection to Water:

Take the small bowl of water and hold it in your hands.

Feel a deep connection with the element of water, which represents emotions, intuition, and flow.

Envision the water cleansing and purifying your intuitive channels.

Crystal Activation:

Hold the amethyst or clear quartz crystal in your hands.

Close your eyes and focus on the crystal's energy, allowing it to align with your intuition and open your third eye.

Visualize the crystal radiating a bright light that clears any blockages and enhances your intuitive abilities.

Written Affirmation:

On the piece of paper or parchment, write down affirmations or positive statements related to your intuition or the guidance you seek.

For example: "I trust my intuition and inner guidance," "I am open to receiving clear messages from the divine," or "I embrace my intuitive gifts and use them for my highest good."

Charging the Affirmation:

Hold the written affirmation in your hands and visualize the energy of intuition and divine guidance infusing the words on the paper.

Read the affirmations aloud, putting your intention and energy into each statement.

Optional Herbal or Divination Tool Use:

If you have chosen to work with intuition-enhancing herbs or divination tools, incorporate them into the spell according to your preference.

You can burn herbs to purify the space or use divination tools to gain insights and guidance.

Affirmation Activation:

Dip the written affirmation into the bowl of water, allowing the water to absorb the energy of your intentions.

Place the activated affirmation under the lit candle or near the crystal, creating a sacred space for intuitive energies.

Closing the Ritual:

Express gratitude to yourself, the divine, or any deities or spirits you work with, acknowledging the gift of intuition and guidance in your life.

Blow out the candle, releasing the energy into the universe.

Take a moment to reflect on the energy you have invoked and the potential for deepening your intuitive connection.

Intuition spells are personal and should align with your own beliefs and desires. Trust in your inner wisdom and the guidance you receive, allowing your intuition to guide you on your spiritual journey.

Chapter Forty-Five

Wiccan Dream Protection Spell

A Wiccan Dream Protection Spell is a ritual performed to safeguard your dreams, ensuring restful sleep, warding off nightmares, and promoting positive and meaningful dream experiences. This spell aims to create a protective barrier around your subconscious mind, allowing you to explore the dream realm with a sense of security and empowerment.

Ingredients:
White candle (representing purity, clarity, and protection)
Small bowl of salt
Lavender essential oil or dried lavender flowers
Piece of amethyst or clear quartz crystal
Piece of paper or parchment
Pen or marker
Altar or sacred space

Preparation:

Find a quiet and sacred space where you can perform the spell without distractions.

Set up your altar or clean surface with your materials.

Take a few moments to ground yourself and enter a calm and focused state of mind.

Setting Your Intention:

Take the piece of paper or parchment and write down your intention for dream protection.

Be clear and specific about what you desire, such as peaceful sleep, protection from nightmares, or vivid and insightful dreams.

Visualize yourself surrounded by a protective energy that shields and guides your dream experiences.

Candle Preparation:

Light the white candle, symbolizing purity, clarity, and protection.

Hold the candle in your hands, infusing it with your intention and the energy of dream protection.

State your intention for the spell, either silently or aloud, such as: "I invoke the energy of protection to safeguard my dreams and promote positive experiences."

Protection Salt:

Take a small pinch of salt from the bowl and hold it in your hand.

Visualize the salt as a purifying and protective substance that repels negative energies and entities from your dream space.

Sprinkle a circle of salt around your candle or around your sleeping area, creating a symbolic barrier of protection.

Lavender Blessing:

If you have lavender essential oil, place a drop on your finger and gently rub it onto your forehead, heart, and wrists.

If you have dried lavender flowers, hold them in your hands and take a moment to connect with their calming and soothing properties.

Inhale the scent of lavender, allowing it to relax your mind and promote a peaceful state.

Crystal Empowerment:

Hold the amethyst or clear quartz crystal in your hands.

Close your eyes and imagine the crystal emitting a soft, protective light.

Envision this light forming a shield around your mind as you sleep, creating a safe and secure dream space.

Written Affirmation:

On the piece of paper or parchment, write down affirmations or positive statements related to dream protection and positive dream experiences.

For example: "My dreams are protected and filled with light," "I have restful and meaningful sleep," or "My dreams offer insights and guidance."

Charging the Affirmation:

Hold the written affirmation in your hands and visualize the energy of protection and positive dream experiences infusing the words on the paper.

Read the affirmations aloud, putting your intention and energy into each statement.

Affirmation Activation:

Place the activated affirmation under the lit candle or near the crystal, symbolizing the integration of your intention with the candle's energy and the crystal's protective properties.

Closing the Ritual:

Express gratitude to yourself, the divine, or any deities or spirits you work with, acknowledging the protection and guidance you seek in your dream realm.

Allow the candle to burn out naturally or extinguish it while expressing gratitude and releasing the energy into the universe.

This spell serves to enhance your dream experiences and provide protection, but it is always important to address any underlying issues or seek professional help if you consistently experience troubling or distressing dreams. Trust in the power of your intention and the support of the divine as you embark on a restful and enlightening dream journey.

Chapter Forty-Six

Wiccan Job or Career Spell

A Wiccan Job or Career Spell is a ritual performed to attract opportunities, success, and fulfillment in your professional life. This spell aims to align your energy with your desired career path, enhance your skills and qualifications, and draw in favorable circumstances for job hunting or advancement. It can be performed when seeking a new job, a promotion, or general career growth. Here are the ingredients and instructions for a basic Wiccan Job or Career Spell:

Ingredients:
Green candle (representing prosperity, abundance, and career growth)
Bay leaf or piece of paper
Pen or marker
Small bowl of salt
Patchouli essential oil or dried patchouli leaves
Clear quartz crystal
Altar or sacred space

Preparation:

Find a quiet and sacred space where you can perform the spell without distractions.

Set up your altar or clean surface with your materials.

Take a moment to center yourself and visualize the career or job you desire, envisioning yourself successful and fulfilled.

Setting Your Intention

Take the bay leaf or piece of paper and write down your intention for your job or career.

Be specific and clear about your goals and desires, such as the type of job, the level of success, or the skills you wish to enhance.

Visualize yourself thriving in your desired career, feeling a sense of fulfillment and abundance.

Candle Preparation:

Light the green candle, symbolizing prosperity, abundance, and career growth.

Hold the candle in your hands, infusing it with your intention and the energy of a successful career.

State your intention for the spell, either silently or aloud, such as: "I attract fulfilling opportunities and success in my career path."

Salt Purification:

Take a pinch of salt from the bowl and sprinkle it over the bay leaf or piece of paper, purifying and cleansing your intention.

Visualize the salt removing any obstacles or negative energies that may hinder your career growth.

Patchouli Empowerment:

If you have patchouli essential oil, place a drop on your finger and rub it onto your wrists or pulse points.

If you have dried patchouli leaves, hold them in your hands and take a moment to connect with their grounding and attracting properties.

Inhale the scent of patchouli, allowing it to uplift your spirits and enhance your confidence and magnetism.

Crystal Activation:

Hold the clear quartz crystal in your hands.

Close your eyes and imagine the crystal amplifying your intentions and radiating positive energy.

Envision it as a magnet for attracting opportunities and abundance in your career.

Written Affirmation:

On the bay leaf or piece of paper, write down affirmations or positive statements related to your job or career aspirations.

For example: "I am skilled and qualified for my dream job," "Opportunities align with my passion and purpose," or "I attract abundance and success in my career."

Charging the Affirmation:

Hold the written affirmation in your hands and visualize the energy of success and fulfillment infusing the words on the leaf or paper.

Read the affirmations aloud, putting your intention and energy into each statement.

Affirmation Activation:

Hold the activated affirmation over the lit candle, allowing the flame to energize and empower your intentions.

Visualize the flame carrying your desires into the universe, igniting the path to your dream career.

Closing the Ritual:

Express gratitude to yourself, the divine, or any deities or spirits you work with, acknowledging the support and guidance you seek in your job or career endeavors.

Allow the candle to burn out naturally or extinguish it while expressing gratitude and releasing the energy into the universe.

While performing a job or career spell can enhance your energy and align you with opportunities, it is essential to take practical steps in your job search or career development. Combine this spell with actions such as networking, updating your resume, and actively pursuing job openings to maximize your chances of success. Trust in the power of your intention and the support of the universe as you manifest a fulfilling and prosperous career.

Chapter Forty-Seven

Wiccan Breaking Bad Habits Spell

A Wiccan Breaking Bad Habits Spell is a ritual performed to help release and overcome negative habits or patterns that no longer serve your highest good. This spell aims to empower you with the strength, determination, and willpower to break free from unhealthy behaviors and embrace positive change. It can be used to address a wide range of habits, such as smoking, overeating, procrastination, or negative thinking.

Ingredients:
Black candle (representing transformation, release, and banishing)
Small piece of paper or parchment
Pen or marker
Salt or black salt
Lemon or lemon essential oil
Small fireproof dish or bowl
Altar or sacred space

Preparation:

Find a quiet and sacred space where you can perform the spell without distractions.

Set up your altar or clean surface with your materials.

Take a moment to reflect on the habit you wish to break and the positive changes you want to manifest in your life.

Setting Your Intention:

Take the piece of paper or parchment and write down your intention for breaking the bad habit.

Be specific and clear about the habit you wish to release and the new behaviors or patterns you want to embrace.

Visualize yourself free from the habit, experiencing a sense of empowerment and personal growth.

Candle Preparation:

Light the black candle, symbolizing transformation, release, and banishing.

Hold the candle in your hands, infusing it with your intention and the energy of breaking free from the negative habit.

State your intention for the spell, either silently or aloud, such as: "I release the hold of [bad habit] and embrace positive change in my life."

Salt Cleansing:

Take a small pinch of salt or black salt and sprinkle it over the piece of paper or parchment, purifying and cleansing your intention.

Visualize the salt absorbing and neutralizing the negative energy associated with the habit.

Lemon Cleansing:

Cut the lemon in half or place a drop of lemon essential oil on your fingertips.

Rub the lemon or lemon-scented oil onto your wrists or pulse points, symbolizing a fresh start and purification of your energy.

Inhale the scent of lemon, allowing it to invigorate and uplift your spirit.

Written Affirmation:

On the piece of paper or parchment, write down affirmations or positive statements related to breaking the bad habit and embracing positive change.

For example: "I release [bad habit] and welcome health and vitality," "I am strong and capable of positive transformation," or "I replace negative habits with empowering choices."

Charging the Affirmation:

Hold the written affirmation in your hands and visualize the energy of transformation and empowerment infusing the words on the paper.

Read the affirmations aloud, putting your intention and energy into each statement.

Affirmation Activation:

Hold the activated affirmation over the flame of the black candle, allowing the fire to transform and release the negative energy associated with the bad habit.

Be careful not to let the paper catch fire. Hold it close enough to the flame to activate the intention but ensure it doesn't burn.

Burning Ritual:

Place the activated affirmation into the fireproof dish or bowl.

As the paper burns, visualize the habit disintegrating and being replaced by positive energy and healthy choices.

Feel a sense of liberation and empowerment as the flames consume the paper.

Closing the Ritual:

Express gratitude to yourself, the divine, or any deities or spirits you work with, acknowledging the support and guidance you seek in breaking the bad habit.

Allow the candle to burn out naturally or extinguish it while expressing gratitude and releasing the energy into the universe.

Breaking a bad habit requires commitment, perseverance, and self-discipline. While a Wiccan Breaking Bad Habits Spell can provide energetic support, it is essential to take practical steps and implement strategies that help you overcome the habit. Combine this spell with actions such as setting clear goals, creating a support system, and developing healthy coping mechanisms to maximize your success. Trust in the power of your intention and the support of the universe as you embrace positive change and personal growth.

Chapter Forty-Eight

Wiccan Creativity Spell

A Wiccan Creativity Spell is a ritual performed to enhance your creative abilities, unlock inspiration, and tap into your artistic potential. This spell aims to connect you with the divine source of creativity, remove blocks or self-doubt, and ignite your imagination. Whether you are an artist, writer, musician, or simply seeking to enhance your creative expression, this spell can help you access your creative flow.

Ingredients:

Purple candle (representing inspiration, intuition, and artistic energy)
Creative tools or materials relevant to your chosen artistic medium (e.g., paintbrushes, musical instrument, writing journal)
Clear quartz crystal
Jasmine or lavender essential oil (or dried jasmine or lavender flowers)
Altar or sacred space

Preparation:

Find a quiet and sacred space where you can perform the spell without distractions.

Set up your altar or clean surface with your materials.

Take a moment to center yourself and focus on your desire to enhance your creativity and artistic expression.

Setting Your Intention:

Hold the creative tools or materials in your hands and connect with the energy of your chosen artistic medium.

Visualize yourself immersed in a state of creative flow, feeling inspired and connected to your inner artist.

State your intention for the spell, either silently or aloud, such as: "I unlock my creative potential and invite inspiration to flow freely."

Candle Preparation:

Light the purple candle, symbolizing inspiration, intuition, and artistic energy.

Hold the candle in your hands, infusing it with your intention and the energy of creative expression.

State your intention for the spell, either silently or aloud, focusing on your desire to enhance your creativity.

Crystal Activation:

Hold the clear quartz crystal in your hands.

Close your eyes and imagine the crystal amplifying your creative energy and connecting you with the divine source of inspiration.

Envision it as a conduit for channeling artistic ideas and expressions.

Scent Activation:

If you have jasmine or lavender essential oil, place a drop on your fingertips and gently rub them together.

If you have dried jasmine or lavender flowers, hold them in your hands and take a moment to connect with their calming and inspiring properties.

Inhale the scent of jasmine or lavender, allowing it to relax your mind and stimulate your senses.

Creative Invocation:

Take your creative tools or materials and set them before the lit candle.

Close your eyes and visualize a radiant purple light surrounding you and your creative space.

Call upon the divine source of creativity and any artistic deities or spirits you resonate with, inviting their guidance and inspiration.

Creative Expression:

Pick up your creative tools or materials and allow your intuition to guide your artistic expression.

Engage in your chosen artistic activity, whether it's painting, playing music, writing, or any other creative endeavor.

Let go of self-judgment or perfectionism and allow the energy to flow naturally.

Affirmations:

As you create, repeat positive affirmations related to your creativity and artistic abilities.

For example: "I am a vessel of divine inspiration," "My creativity flows effortlessly and abundantly," or "I embrace my unique artistic expression."

Crystal Charging:

Place the clear quartz crystal near your creative workspace or hold it in your hand as you continue your creative process.

Visualize the crystal absorbing the energy of your creative flow, amplifying your inspiration, and helping you bring forth your best artistic expression.

Closing the Ritual:

Express gratitude to yourself, the divine, or any artistic deities or spirits you called upon, acknowledging their support and the creative energy you have invoked.

Allow the candle to burn out naturally or extinguish it while expressing gratitude and releasing the energy into the universe.

A Wiccan Creativity Spell is a tool to enhance your creative energy, but the true power lies within you. Embrace your unique artistic expression and trust in your creative abilities. Combine this spell with regular creative practices, seeking inspiration from nature and other artists, and nurturing your creativity through self-care and self-expression. Trust in the power of your intention and the support of the universe as you tap into your creative flow and unleash your artistic potential.

Chapter Forty-Nine

Wiccan Travel Protection Spell

A Wiccan Travel Protection Spell is a ritual performed to ensure safe and protected travels, whether you're embarking on a short journey or a long-distance trip. This spell aims to create a shield of protection around you, ward off negative energies, and attract positive experiences during your travels. It can be used for any mode of transportation, including air travel, road trips, or even walking journeys.

Ingredients:
Blue candle (representing protection, calm, and safe travels)
Small piece of paper or parchment
Pen or marker
Protective herbs or essential oils (such as lavender, rosemary, or basil)
Clear quartz crystal
Small pouch or bag
Altar or sacred space

Preparation:

Find a quiet and sacred space where you can perform the spell without distractions.

Set up your altar or clean surface with your materials.

Take a moment to center yourself and focus on your upcoming travel, visualizing a safe and protected journey.

Setting Your Intention:

Hold the blue candle in your hands, connecting with its energy of protection and safe travels.

State your intention for the spell, either silently or aloud, such as: "I invoke the energies of protection to surround me during my travels, ensuring safety and positive experiences."

Candle Preparation:

Light the blue candle, symbolizing protection, calm, and safe travels.

Hold the candle in your hands, infusing it with your intention and the energy of protection.

State your intention for the spell, either silently or aloud, focusing on your desire for safe and protected travels.

Written Protection Statement:

Take the piece of paper or parchment and write down a statement of protection for your travels.

Be specific and clear about the type of protection you seek, such as protection from accidents, delays, or negative energies.

Fold the paper or parchment and hold it between your palms, infusing it with your intention and the energy of protection.

Herb or Oil Activation:

Take a pinch of the protective herbs or a few drops of the essential oils on your fingertips.

Rub the herbs or oils onto the candle, coating it with their protective properties.

Visualize a shield of energy forming around the candle, radiating protective vibrations.

Crystal Charging:

Hold the clear quartz crystal in your hands and close your eyes.

Visualize the crystal absorbing the energy of protection and amplifying it.

State your intention for the crystal, such as: "I charge this crystal to enhance the protective energy surrounding me during my travels."

Protection Infusion:

Lightly touch the folded paper or parchment with the charged crystal, infusing it with the protective energy.

Visualize the protective energy enveloping the paper, forming a shield of protection around you during your travels.

Placing in the Pouch:

Carefully place the activated paper or parchment into the small pouch or bag.

If desired, you can add additional protective herbs or crystals to the pouch for extra reinforcement.

Carrying the Pouch:

Keep the pouch close to you during your travels, such as in your bag, pocket, or worn as jewelry.

Touch the pouch or hold it in your hands whenever you need an extra sense of protection or reassurance.

Closing the Ritual:

Express gratitude to yourself, the divine, or any deities or spirits you work with, acknowledging their support and the protection you seek in your travels.

Allow the candle to burn out naturally or extinguish it while expressing gratitude and releasing the protective energy into the universe.

A Wiccan Travel Protection Spell is a tool to enhance your sense of safety and well-being during your travels, but it's also important to take practical precautions and follow any necessary travel guidelines. Trust in the power of your intention, the protection of the universe, and your own intuition as you embark on your journey. Safe travels!

Chapter Fifty

Wiccan Ancestral Connection Spell

A Wiccan Ancestral Connection Spell is a ritual performed to honor and connect with your ancestors, seeking their guidance, wisdom, and support. This spell aims to create a sacred space where you can communicate with your ancestral spirits and strengthen your connection to your lineage. By tapping into the ancestral energy, you can gain insights, receive blessings, and cultivate a deeper understanding of your roots.

Ingredients:
White candle (representing purity, clarity, and spiritual connection)
Ancestral altar or sacred space
Photos or mementos of your ancestors
Incense or herbs associated with ancestral communication (such as sage, rosemary, or mugwort)
A journal or piece of paper
Pen or marker
Optional: Offering items for your ancestors (such as food, drink, or symbolic items)

Preparation:

Find a quiet and sacred space where you can perform the spell without distractions.

Set up your ancestral altar or clean surface with your materials.

Gather photos or mementos of your ancestors, arranging them in a respectful manner.

Take a moment to center yourself and focus on your intention to connect with your ancestors and honor their presence.

Setting Your Intention:

Light the white candle, symbolizing purity, clarity, and spiritual connection.

Hold the candle in your hands, infusing it with your intention and the energy of ancestral connection.

State your intention for the spell, either silently or aloud, such as: "I open myself to the wisdom and guidance of my ancestors. I seek their presence and blessings."

Ancestral Invocation:

Take a few deep breaths and visualize a soft white light surrounding you and your sacred space.

Call upon your ancestors, inviting their presence into the ritual.

You can address them by saying something like: "Ancestors of my bloodline, I call upon you with respect and love. Please join me in this sacred space."

Incense or Herb Activation:

Light the incense or herbs associated with ancestral communication, allowing the smoke to fill the air.

As the smoke rises, visualize it carrying your intentions and messages to your ancestors, creating a bridge between the physical and spiritual realms.

Ancestral Connection Meditation:

Close your eyes and enter a meditative state.

Visualize yourself surrounded by a loving and supportive presence of your ancestors.

Allow yourself to feel their energy, love, and wisdom flowing towards you.

Take this time to listen, observe, and receive any messages or insights that come to you.

Communication and Offering:

Open your journal or take a piece of paper and write down any thoughts, messages, or feelings that arise during the meditation.

If you have offering items for your ancestors, place them on the altar or near their photos or mementos as a symbolic gesture of gratitude and respect.

Ancestral Guidance:

Spend a few moments in silent reflection, feeling the connection to your ancestors and expressing gratitude for their presence.

Ask for guidance, clarity, or support in any areas of your life where you seek their wisdom.

Closing the Ritual:

Express gratitude to your ancestors, acknowledging their presence, guidance, and the connection you've established.

Blow out the candle to signify the closing of the ritual, while expressing your thanks and releasing the energy into the universe.

A Wiccan Ancestral Connection Spell is a sacred act of honoring and communing with your ancestors. Approach this spell with reverence, respect, and an open heart. Cultivate a regular practice of ancestral connection, allowing the bond with your lineage to deepen over time. Trust in the wisdom, love, and guidance that your ancestors can offer as you navigate your life's journey

Chapter Fifty-One

Wiccan Empowerment Spell

A Wiccan Empowerment Spell is a ritual performed to boost your personal power, self-confidence, and inner strength. This spell aims to help you tap into your own potential, embrace your unique gifts, and step into your authentic power. By harnessing the energy of the elements and connecting with the divine forces within and around you, this spell can assist you in cultivating a sense of empowerment and courage.

Ingredients:
Yellow or gold candle (representing personal power and confidence)
Altar or sacred space
Crystal or stone associated with empowerment (such as citrine, tiger's eye, or carnelian)
A piece of paper or parchment
Pen or marker
Incense or herbs associated with empowerment (such as frankincense, cinnamon, or ginger)
Optional: Items representing your personal strengths or symbols of empowerment

Preparation:

Find a quiet and sacred space where you can perform the spell without distractions.

Set up your altar or clean surface with your materials.

Take a moment to center yourself and focus on your intention to cultivate empowerment and embrace your inner strength.

Setting Your Intention:

Light the yellow or gold candle, symbolizing personal power and confidence.

Hold the candle in your hands, infusing it with your intention and the energy of empowerment.

State your intention for the spell, either silently or aloud, such as: "I embrace my personal power and step into my authentic strength. I am empowered in all areas of my life."

Crystal Activation:

Hold the chosen crystal or stone in your hands and close your eyes.

Take a few deep breaths and visualize the crystal being filled with a bright, empowering light.

State your intention for the crystal, such as: "I activate this crystal to amplify my personal power and infuse me with courage and confidence."

Empowerment Affirmation:

Take the piece of paper or parchment and write down an affirmation that resonates with your desired sense of empowerment.

Be specific and use positive language to affirm your personal power and abilities.

For example: "I am confident, strong, and capable. I embrace my unique gifts and shine brightly in all that I do."

Read the affirmation aloud, allowing its words to resonate within you.

Incense or Herb Activation:

Light the incense or herbs associated with empowerment, allowing the smoke to fill the air.

As the smoke rises, visualize it carrying your intentions and affirmations, surrounding you with a sense of empowerment and strength.

Self-Empowerment Ritual:

Take a moment to reflect on your personal strengths, talents, and achievements.

If you have any items that represent these qualities or symbols of empowerment, place them on the altar or hold them in your hands as you continue the ritual.

Candle Charging:

Hold the empowered crystal in one hand and the candle in the other.

Pass the candle through the smoke of the incense or herbs, purifying it and infusing it with the energy of empowerment.

Place the crystal near the candle, allowing their energies to merge.

Candle Visualization:

Light the candle, focusing on its flame.

Visualize the flame growing brighter and stronger, representing your own inner power and confidence.

See the flame as a beacon of light, illuminating your path and guiding you towards your goals.

Empowerment Affirmation:

Repeat your chosen affirmation several times, either silently or aloud.

Feel the words resonating within you, reinforcing your sense of personal power and empowerment.

Closing the Ritual:

Express gratitude to the divine forces, your inner strength, and the elements for their presence and assistance.

Blow out the candle, while expressing your thanks and releasing the energy into the universe.

A Wiccan Empowerment Spell is a powerful tool to enhance your sense of personal power and self-confidence. Use this spell as a catalyst to embrace your unique abilities, step into your authentic self, and navigate life with strength and courage. Trust in the power of your intention, the support of the universe, and your own inner wisdom as you empower yourself in all areas of your life.

Chapter Fifty-Two

Wiccan Justice Spell

A Wiccan Justice Spell is a ritual performed to seek fairness, balance, and just outcomes in situations where justice is needed. This spell aims to harness the energies of the universe and call upon the forces of justice to ensure that truth and fairness prevail. It can be used to address conflicts, resolve disputes, or seek retribution for wrongdoings. It is important to approach this spell with a sense of responsibility and integrity, focusing on seeking justice rather than revenge.

Ingredients:
White candle (symbolizing purity, truth, and justice)
Black candle (symbolizing protection and banishment of negativity)
Justice-related herbs or incense (such as sage, frankincense, or myrrh)
A piece of paper or parchment
Pen or marker
An object or symbol representing justice (optional)
Salt (symbolizing purification and grounding)

Preparation:

Find a quiet and sacred space where you can perform the spell without distractions.

Set up your altar or clean surface with your materials.

Take a moment to center yourself and focus on your intention to seek justice and balance.

Setting Your Intention:

Place the white candle on the left side of your altar and the black candle on the right side.

Light the white candle, stating your intention for justice and fairness, such as: "I call upon the energies of justice to prevail in this situation. May truth and fairness guide the outcome."

Banishing Negativity:

Light the black candle, symbolizing the banishment of negativity and unjust influences.

Visualize any negative energies, biases, or unjust intentions being dispelled and replaced with clarity and truth.

Herbal or Incense Activation:

Light the justice-related herbs or incense, allowing the smoke to fill the air.

As the smoke rises, visualize it carrying your intentions for justice, spreading fairness and balance throughout the situation.

Justice Invocation:

Take a moment to reflect on the concept of justice and what it means to you.

Call upon the energies of justice, stating your intention to seek fair outcomes and resolution.

You can say something like: "I invoke the forces of justice to guide this situation. May truth prevail, and fairness be served."

Written Petition:

Take the piece of paper or parchment and write down your desired outcome or justice-related intention.

Be clear and specific in stating what you seek, focusing on the fair resolution of the situation.

Place the written petition on the altar, between the two candles.

Symbolic Object (Optional):

If you have an object or symbol representing justice, place it on the altar near the written petition.

This can be a small figurine, a symbol like the scales of justice, or any item that holds personal significance.

Salt Purification:

Sprinkle a pinch of salt around the written petition and the candles, symbolizing purification and grounding of the energy.

Visualization and Affirmation:

Close your eyes and visualize the situation being resolved in a just and fair manner.

See all parties involved finding a peaceful resolution and receiving fair treatment.

Repeat an affirmation of justice and fairness, such as: "By the powers of justice, balance, and truth, I manifest a just outcome in this situation."

Closing the Ritual:

Express gratitude to the forces of justice, the elements, and any deities or guides you invoked.

Allow the candles to burn out safely or snuff them out, while expressing your thanks and releasing the energy into the universe.

The Wiccan Justice Spell is intended to seek fairness, balance, and just outcomes. Approach this spell with integrity and a genuine desire for justice, rather than seeking revenge or harm. Trust in the power of the universe and the energies you have invoked to guide the situation towards a fair resolution.

Chapter Fifty-Three

Wiccan New Beginnings Spell

A Wiccan New Beginnings Spell is a ritual performed to mark the start of a new chapter in life, whether it's the beginning of a new year, a fresh start after a challenging period, or the initiation of a new project or phase. This spell aims to harness the energies of renewal, transformation, and growth to bring positive changes and opportunities into your life. It is a powerful tool for setting intentions, manifesting new beginnings, and welcoming positive energy.

Ingredients:
White candle (symbolizing purity, clarity, and new beginnings)
Green candle (symbolizing growth, abundance, and prosperity)
A small bowl of water
A small bowl of salt
A piece of paper or parchment
Pen or marker
Fresh flowers or herbs (symbolizing renewal and new growth)
Optional: Crystals or gemstones associated with new beginnings (such as clear quartz or moonstone)

Preparation:

Find a quiet and sacred space where you can perform the spell without distractions.

Set up your altar or clean surface with your materials.

Take a moment to center yourself and reflect on the new beginning you wish to manifest.

Setting Your Intention:

Light the white candle, symbolizing purity and clarity.

Hold your hands over the candle flame and state your intention for the new beginning, such as: "I embrace this new chapter in my life. May it be filled with growth, abundance, and positive opportunities."

Elemental Purification:

Take the bowl of water and sprinkle a few drops over your hands, symbolizing the purifying and cleansing properties of water.

Say: "With this water, I cleanse and purify myself, releasing any past energies that no longer serve my journey."

Symbolic Purification:

Take a pinch of salt from the bowl and sprinkle it over the piece of paper or parchment.

Visualize the salt purifying the paper and removing any obstacles or negative energies.

Say: "With this salt, I cleanse and purify my path, removing any barriers and inviting positive energies for new beginnings."

Written Intention:

Write down your intention for the new beginning on the piece of paper or parchment.

Be specific and clear in stating your desires, focusing on positive and empowering language.

For example: "I welcome new opportunities for personal growth, abundance, and happiness in my life. I am open to positive change and new beginnings."

Candle Activation:

Light the green candle, symbolizing growth, abundance, and prosperity.

Hold the piece of paper with your written intention and pass it through the flame of the green candle, infusing it with the energy of new beginnings.

Visualize your intention manifesting as the flame ignites the transformative power within you.

Floral Offering:

Arrange the fresh flowers or herbs on your altar or hold them in your hands.

Close your eyes and connect with the vibrant energy of the flowers, envisioning them as symbols of renewal and new growth.

Offer the flowers or herbs to the elements, expressing gratitude for the new beginnings you are welcoming.

Crystal Energy (Optional):

If you have chosen crystals or gemstones associated with new beginnings, hold them in your hands or place them on your altar.

Visualize the crystals radiating their energy of transformation and positive change, amplifying your intentions.

Affirmation and Visualization:

Hold the piece of paper with your intention in both hands and read it aloud, infusing it with your energy and conviction.

Close your eyes and visualize yourself stepping into the new beginning, feeling the excitement, growth, and abundance that it brings.

Repeat a positive affirmation aligned with your intention, such as: "I embrace new beginnings with open arms. I am ready to receive the blessings that come my way."

Closing the Ritual:

Express gratitude to the divine forces, the elements, and any deities or guides you invoked.

Allow the candles to burn out safely or snuff them out, while expressing your thanks and releasing the energy into the universe.

Keep the piece of paper with your intention in a safe place or carry it with you as a reminder of your new beginnings.

The Wiccan New Beginnings Spell is a powerful way to set intentions, manifest positive changes, and invite new opportunities into your life. Embrace the energy of renewal, growth, and transformation as you embark on your new journey. Trust in the power of your intentions and the support of the universe to guide you towards a bright and prosperous future.

Chapter Fifty-Four

Wiccan Gratitude Spell

A Wiccan Gratitude Spell is a ritual performed to express gratitude and appreciation for the blessings, abundance, and positive experiences in your life. This spell aims to cultivate an attitude of gratitude and amplify the positive energies around you. It is a powerful tool for shifting your focus to the things you are thankful for and attracting more positivity into your life. Here are the ingredients and instructions for a basic Wiccan Gratitude Spell:

Ingredients:
Yellow candle (symbolizing joy, positivity, and gratitude)
Small bowl or dish
Pen or marker
Pieces of paper or small notecards
A selection of gratitude-related herbs or incense (such as lavender, rosemary, or cinnamon)
Optional: Crystals or gemstones associated with gratitude (such as citrine or rose quartz)

Preparation:

Find a quiet and sacred space where you can perform the spell without distractions.

Set up your altar or clean surface with your materials.

Take a moment to center yourself and reflect on the things you are grateful for.

Setting Your Intention:

Light the yellow candle, symbolizing joy, positivity, and gratitude.

Take a few deep breaths and focus on the flame, allowing its warm glow to fill you with gratitude.

State your intention for the spell, such as: "I express deep gratitude for the blessings in my life. May this spell amplify my sense of gratitude and attract more positivity into my experience."

Gratitude Reflection:

Take a few moments to reflect on the things you are grateful for. Consider your relationships, achievements, experiences, and the simple joys of life.

Allow yourself to fully feel the gratitude and appreciation for each blessing.

Written Gratitude:

Take the pieces of paper or small notecards and write down specific things you are grateful for.

Be as specific and detailed as possible, expressing gratitude for the blessings in your life.

For example: "I am grateful for my loving family, supportive friends, good health, and the opportunities for personal growth that have come my way."

Herb or Incense Activation:

Light the gratitude-related herbs or incense, allowing the aroma to fill the air.

As the scent envelops you, let it remind you of the abundance and blessings that surround you.

Gratitude Offering:

Place the bowl or dish on your altar or hold it in your hands.

Take each written gratitude note and hold it to your heart, infusing it with the energy of gratitude.

Offer the notes to the bowl, one by one, expressing your thanks and appreciation as you do so.

Crystal Energy (Optional):

If you have chosen crystals or gemstones associated with gratitude, hold them in your hands or place them around the bowl.

Visualize the crystals amplifying the energy of gratitude, enhancing your feelings of appreciation and attracting more blessings.

Affirmation and Visualization:

Close your eyes and hold the bowl in your hands.

Repeat a gratitude affirmation, such as: "I am grateful for the abundance in my life. I attract more blessings and positivity as I embrace an attitude of gratitude."

Closing the Ritual:

Express gratitude to the divine forces, the elements, and any deities or guides you invoked.

Allow the candle to burn out safely or snuff it out, while expressing your thanks and releasing the energy into the universe.

Keep the gratitude notes in a special place or carry them with you as a reminder of the blessings in your life.

A Wiccan Gratitude Spell is a powerful way to cultivate an attitude of gratitude and attract more positivity into your life. Take the time to appreciate the blessings you have, both big and small. By expressing gratitude, you open yourself up to receiving more abundance and joy. Embrace the practice of gratitude as a daily ritual and watch as the positive energies flow into your life.

Chapter Fifty-Five

Robert J Dornan Books

All Robert J Dornan books can be found on every major platform and in thousands of libraries. Many are also available in French, Spanish, German, and Tagalog. Available in e-books, paperback, and Audio

Fiction:

23 Minutes Past 1 A.M. (Bestseller)

Gwydion

Lost in Jack City (Coming Soon)

Non-Fiction

Lucky You: The Ultimate Book of Fortune and 100 Spells

Everything You Need to Know About Aries

Everything You Need to Know About Taurus

Everything You Need to Know About Gemini

Everything You Need to Know About the Zodiac Sign Cancer

Everything You Need to Know About Leo

Everything You Need to Know About Virgo

Everything You Need to Know About Libra

Everything You Need to Know About Scorpio

Everything You Need to Know About Sagittarius

Everything You Need to Know About Capricorn

Everything You Need to Know About Aquarius

Everything You Need to Know About Pisces

Everything You Need to Know About the Chinese Sign, Rat

Everything You Need to Know About the Chinese Sign, Ox

Everything You Need to Know About the Chinese Sign, Tiger

Everything You Need to Know About the Chinese Sign, Rabbit

Everything You Need to Know About the Chinese Sign, Dragon

Everything You Need to Know About the Chinese Sign, Snake

Everything You Need to Know About the Chinese Sign, Horse

Everything You Need to Know About the Chinese Sign, Goat

Everything You Need to Know About the Chinese Sign, Monkey

Everything You Need to Know About the Chinese Sign, Rooster

Everything You Need to Know About the Chinese Sign, Dog

Everything You Need to Know About the Chinese Sign, Pig

100 True and Terrifying Ghost Stories

The Great Big Book of Ghosts

50 of History's Most Sinister Demons - Part One

50 Stories and Legends About Vampires

50 Famous Exorcisms

Hexed and Hallowed: The True Story of Witches, Then and Now

For more information, visit https://philippineone.com/shop
or
https://robertjdornanbooks.blogspot.com/

www.ingramcontent.com/pod-product-compliance
Ingram Content Group UK Ltd.
Pitfield, Milton Keynes, MK11 3LW, UK
UKHW040906240225
455493UK00001B/261